The Holy Brothers

Reb Elimelekh of Lizhensk and Reb Zusha of Anipoli

MENORAH

Simcha Raz

THE **HOLY BROTHERS**

Reb Elimelekh of **Lizhensk**
and **Reb Zusha** of **Anipoli**

The Lieberman Family Edition

Translated by
Dov Peretz Elkins

Menorah Books

The Holy Brothers
Reb Elimelekh of Lizhensk and Reb Zusha of Anipoli

First English Edition, 2019

Menorah Books
An imprint of Koren Publishers Jerusalem Ltd.

POB 8531, New Milford, CT 06776-8531, USA
& POB 4044, Jerusalem 9104001, Israel
www.menorahbooks.com

The publication of this book was made possible through
the generous support of *Beth Oloth Canada*.

ISBN 978-1-940516-84-4, *hardcover*

A CIP catalogue record for this title is
available from the British Library

Printed and bound in the United States

In memory of
Eliezer & Reizel Lieberman, *z"l*
and their sons,
Aron Lieberman, *z"l*
Leibish Lieberman, *z"l*
Sam Lieberman, *z"l*

Born in Lizhensk, Poland, in the town of Reb Elimelekh, our grandparents and fathers escaped the horrors of Europe through Siberia and reached Montreal, Canada, where the family settled and prospered.

They were dedicated in every way to their families, and their families to them. They were renowned for their kindness, their commitment to Torah and mitzvot, and their generosity to all who turned to them for help and support.

In honor of my beloved mother – Sora Eisenberg Landes

And my cherished sisters – Rena Landes Rank, Rebecca Landes, and Tamar Landes

GREAT Jewish women all!

With love and pride,

Joshua H. Landes

Contents

Foreword

Rabbi Hanoch Teller

According to legend, the Baal Shem Tov, the founder of the Hasidic Movement, was able to go to a specific spot in the forest, recite a particular formula, and an angel appeared.

One generation later, they knew the exact spot where the Baal Shem Tov was able to invoke the appearance of an angel, but they knew not what to say, and an angel did not appear.

And one generation later, they were no longer certain as to the precise spot that the Baal Shem would frequent.

And we, so many generations later and removed, we do not even know where the forest is, let alone the formula that he would recite. What do we have of the grandeur and majesty of the Baal Shem Tov?

We have a lot, for we have the story, and the story takes us back.

The stories of the holy brothers, Reb Elimelekh and Reb Zusha, bring us back, back to a time where there was no pretentiousness or personal agendas – just a simple life where serving the Lord with simplicity and sincerity was supreme, as was love of your fellow Jew – regardless of his or her station in life or observance.

At the time of the holy brothers in the mid-eighteenth century, the Jews in Poland worked for the unusually cruel feudal lords, each of whom they referred to as the *poritz*. Invariably, the *poritzes* were interested in squeezing and extorting whatever money they could out of the Jews, and mercilessly punished, with full government endorsement, any delinquency in tax or rent.

One of the many Jews who had incurred the wrath of his *poritz* had an outstanding debt of three thousand golden coins. It was off to prison for him, and the *poritz* made it very clear that the inmate would never see the light of day again until his debt was fully repaid, and this was not a vain threat.

Kindhearted and benevolent, Reb Eliezer Lipman learned of this poor soul's plight and sought to redeem him from captivity. It would be an august challenge, for he had only a thousand golden coins. Still, he did not falter in his quest and went to speak with the *poritz.*

As he was making his way to the *poritz*'s doorstep he heard torturous moans, which he gathered were from the Jewish prisoner held in the mansion's dungeon. Those awful moans only further strengthened Reb Eliezer's resolve.

The visitor was ushered into the home of the *poritz,* who was cordial until he learned the purpose of the call. Any trace of geniality evaporated at the very mention of the prisoner. "The stinking Jew owes me three thousand golden coins," the *poritz* fumed, "for all of the time that he hasn't paid his debts. He will rot in the cell to the last of his days until every coin is received!"

Reb Eliezer attempted to reason with the coldhearted land owner. "What have you to gain from a tenant who dies in jail? You are after your money, and this will not return it. Let me pay you all the money that I have, a thousand golden coins, for the freedom of the detainee, and surely the Lord will bless you so that you will not lose out from this deal."

But the *poritz* would not budge. However, Reb Eliezer also would not give up. Finally, the determined philanthropist prevailed, and the inmate was released.

The *poritz* was impressed both by Reb Eliezer's negotiations, and that a perfect stranger would spend a thousand coins of his own money to redeem a fellow Jew. "I see that you are an upright man," the *poritz* commented, "and I am therefore going to offer you a break. Since you are a flax merchant, I recommend that you travel to my brother-in-law, who is a flax distributor. I will write you a letter of recommendation encouraging him to give you a substantial discount."

"Thank you," Reb Eliezer responded softly, "but I parted with my last coin in order to redeem your captive."

"In that case," reflected the *poritz*, "here is your money back; invest it wisely with my brother-in-law!"

Joyously, Reb Eliezer departed to the flax distributor armed with his letter of recommendation. The new *poritz* read the letter and was amenable to make a sale at a fair price. He had Reb Eliezer escorted to his warehouse where he could personally inspect the low-cost, quality material.

Just as they were leaving the warehouse, Reb Eliezer heard a tormented shriek from somewhere nearby. "What is that noise?" he wanted to know.

"Oh that," the worker said with a flip of his hand. "It's hard to believe that old Jewish farmhand is still alive. Ever since he was imprisoned he has made such a racket that we have denied him food and drink to quiet him down. Eventually, I guess, it will work…"

Upon hearing this, Reb Eliezer dropped the flax in his hands and rushed out of the warehouse to speak with the man he had just negotiated with. Using the money that he had brought for his purchase, Eliezer Lipman managed to redeem the prisoner.

The captive was released in a dreadful state and Reb Eliezer had a doctor summoned and food gingerly administered. He then invited the man to come to his house for the holiday of Passover that was approaching.

Grateful that he had managed to save a fellow Jew before it was too late, Eliezer and his guest were about to set off when the wholesaler called out, "Hey, what about our deal? Don't you wish to purchase some flax?"

"How could I ever do business with a man as wicked as you?" Reb Eliezer declared. "Have you no compassion or human dignity?"

Most amazingly, this *poritz* was visibly moved by the reproof. Filled with contrition, he pledged that from that day forward he would never commit a shameful act, and to prove his intentions he reduced his price even more and put the money for the ransom toward the flax purchase.

Eliezer Lipman was amazed how things had developed. It was exactly as the Rabbis had taught: one mitzva brings in its train another mitzva! Both ransoms did not cost him, fulfilling the rabbinic teaching that no action or mitzva ever goes unrewarded.

But what greater reward could Eliezer have received for his constant kindness and charity than a beautiful family, two of his sons being none other than Reb Elimelekh of Lizhensk and Reb Zusha of Anipoli?

The parents of the holy brothers, as they came to be known, Eliezer Lipman and his pious wife Mirish, were descended from families that could trace their lineage all the way back to Rashi, Rav Yochanan HaSandlar of talmudic fame, and even King David. They lived in the townlet of Lapachi, not far from Tiktin.

As Mirish was illiterate in the Holy Tongue, she would recite her blessings by heart. Reb Zusha testified that at the time that his mother prayed, the Divine Presence could be found in the home. Every Friday before Sabbath she would travel to Tiktin to dispense alms.

The day that the Baal Shem Tov visited Eliezer and Mirish's village marked a turning point in their lives. From then on, they faithfully provided candles to the synagogue, and were meticulous in prayer as they beseeched the Almighty to open the hearts of their four sons and one daughter to the Torah.

After the passing of Eliezer Lipman, his sons divided their father's inheritance in the following manner: Avraham received the cash and the house was given to Nosson. The jewelry and housewares went to Elimelekh and the outstanding debts were to be collected by Zusha.

The division had been contrived by Zusha, who was clever at disguising his intentions. He made it appear that he had time on his hands, and accordingly, was the most suited for this least desirous of portions: the collection of debts.

However, Zusha was in no way cut out for this mission, and without a penny from the inheritance was left destitute. Bereft of any means of support, he decided to travel to his uncle who was an assistant to the holy Maggid of Mezritch, the successor of the Baal Shem Tov.

Lodging with his uncle meant constant exposure to the Maggid, and in no time, Zusha became an ardent Hasid. In the meantime, Elimelekh had moved to his wife's hometown of Shineva.

After his stay with his uncle in Mezritch, Zusha departed for the home of his brother Elimelekh. The very long and arduous journey took its toll on Zusha's attire. His worn-out tatters were far shabbier than those that clad the poorest beggars.

Ever vigilant of the honor of his in-laws, Elimelekh was ashamed to allow his dreadfully appearing brother into his home. He therefore arranged accommodations for him at the home of the local baker.

However, Zusha's nights were not earmarked for mundane sleep. Those precious hours were devoted to learning, prayer and the loud recitation of *tikkun ḥatzot*. Zusha's nocturnal agenda effectively brought an end to his tenancy at the baker's house, and Elimelekh had no recourse other than to invite his brother into his own home.

It was there that he was able to observe Zusha's ways firsthand, which awakened in him a desire to draw close to the Maggid of Mezritch. Reb Zusha also convinced his older brother to join him in a self-imposed exile which they would devote to elevating the people that they would encounter.

Attired in the clothes of exile, they would travel from village to village to persuade, direct, and inspire the people to desist from sin and return to their holy roots. The exile would also, as the Talmud teaches, purify their souls.

And indeed, across the length and breadth of the Polish landscape the brothers wandered, bringing the word of the Lord to those that were either unfamiliar or needed to be reminded. The holy brothers, in a manner all their own, made focusing upon God a central part of people's lives.

Wherever the two holy brothers went during their self-imposed exile they generated a spirit of repentance. Their standard routine was to admonish themselves out loud for their supposed crimes, when in fact their "sins" were precisely the ones that the villager within earshot needed to rectify.

"Melekh, Melekh," Reb Elimelekh would reprimand himself, "how will you ever be able to face your final judgment knowing that you took advantage of your customers' naiveté?"

"I am certainly no better," Reb Zusha would add. "How could I have avoided davening with a minyan?" he mourned.

The two of them used their clairvoyant abilities to determine exactly what it was that the locals had transgressed, and then elaborated as to how they would personally be punished for those very same sins. Invariably, this caused the true sinners to be filled with remorse and rectify their sinful deeds. Countless individuals improved their lives this way without having their dignity compromised or having been humiliated in the process.

Wandering from town to village, the holy brothers neglected their physical needs and were sustained solely by meager coins or scraps of food that were donated along the way. One Sunday night they found themselves in a new town on a cold, wintry night. The tavern keeper offered to lodge them behind the fireplace that heated the pub.

The two of them took their places on the floor, with Reb Zusha, as always, offering his older brother the preferred spot nearer the fire. No sooner had Reb Elimelekh and Reb Zusha settled down to rest their weary bones when the tavern began to fill up with locals who had come to celebrate nothing more than their inebriated state. Wobbling and singing as drunkards do, they made themselves merry until they stumbled across a *real* cause for celebration.

Right before their eyes, innocently sleeping on the floor, was a Jew who could serve as the evening's entertainment. As many of them were wagon drivers, they were equipped with whips and staffs that could readily enlist the sleeping Jew's cooperation.

"Up and dance!" they ordered, snapping their whips and beating their staffs to ensure immediate compliance. Reb Zusha sprang to his feet and danced energetically for the leering drunkards. The wagon drivers were not looking for a quick performance – they had all night – and they unsparingly utilized their appurtenances to assure protracted amusement.

Eventually, however, they grew tired and allowed Zusha to collapse on the floor. But it wasn't just *one* Jew that they had savagely beaten. Reb Elimelekh felt every blow on his *own* back and urgently pressed his brother to exchange places with him. "They'll be back and then it will be my turn to suffer their indignities."

But in no way did Reb Zusha feel that he was getting the worst of the deal. Being beaten simply because he was a defenseless Jew was good for the soul, he maintained. And he knew his brother did not dispute this point.

Still, Reb Elimelekh would have none of it. He was insistent that they switch places so that if the drunks decided again to be entertained, *he* would bear the brunt of their vile behavior.

And indeed the wagon drivers returned, eager for another dance performance. Not for naught had they entered the tavern.

But in a display of uncharacteristic egalitarianism, they announced that it would only be fair to wake the Jew lying nearer to the fireplace, for the outer one had already made his contribution to the night's festivities.

Reb Elimelekh stood up and explained, or at least *tried* to explain, that the *outer* Jew was previously the *inner* one, for they had switched places. But his entreaties fell upon drunken ears.

Reb Zusha sanguinely accepted his lot and commented, "Melekh, don't feel bad. You see that one who deserves to be beaten cannot avoid it. Your desire to switch places was willed from Heaven."

Eventually the wagon drivers tired of their entertainment and they crashed to the floor in a drunken stupor. The brothers arose to recite *tikkun ḥatzot* and to thank the Almighty for having separated them from inhumane derelicts. Blessed were they to be servants privileged to worship the Almighty.

The holy brothers never forgot those that extended themselves on their behalf in their period of exile. One such individual was Reb Aharon in the village of Ludmir, who served as their host whenever they visited the town. Reb Aharon lived in abject poverty, but this never stopped him from extending hospitality and sharing his meager crumbs.

Once Reb Elimelekh and Reb Zusha were revealed as famous tzaddikim, and their followers were everywhere to be found, they returned to Ludmir – this time in a horse-drawn carriage. Just as in the past, they turned to Reb Aharon for lodging, which he graciously offered, as always.

Overnight, Reb Aharon's modest hovel became the focus of the town, and masses formed outside the door to seek the tzaddikim's blessings and intervention in a host of matters.

One of the wealthy merchants in the town felt that *he* deserved the honor of hosting these famous guests, and he extended his invitation for them to come to his richly appointed house where they could dwell in perfect comfort. But the brothers flatly refused.

"What is the difference between our visit this time," the brothers wanted to know, "and our earlier visits, when you did not extend us an invitation? We are the very same people; just this time we came with a horse and wagon.

"We therefore propose that you host the horse and wagon..."

In the court of the Maggid, Reb Elimelekh was considered one of the finest students. And when the great Maggid's soul was summoned above, the disciples gathered to decide upon his successor. The consensus was that there was a need for a leader that was robust and energetic, articulate and charismatic, who would know how to watch over his flock and even, if necessary, engage in battle on behalf of the Hasidic Movement. Once these guidelines were established, the question of who would succeed became a moot one.

Unanimously the disciples elected to crown Reb Elimelekh with the mantle of leadership to direct and spread *Ḥasidut* in Poland and Galicia. Upon reaching their decision they chanted in unison, "*Yeḥi adonenu v'rabbenu* – Long live our master and teacher, Reb Elimelekh!"

From there the group of Hasidim departed to Lizhensk with Reb Elimelekh at the head of the procession. The group continued until evening descended and it was necessary to lodge for the night. They entered an inn along the way and requested a single room for their newly appointed master.

To the great astonishment of the Hasidim, Reb Elimelekh requested pillows and covers from the innkeeper – as if he were planning to retire for the *entire* night. Several hours later the Hasidim were, well, appalled that their new master was still sleeping like a commoner. The Maggid who had preceded him had never allowed himself more than a few hours of sleep. Without anyone saying a word, there was a profound sense of regret over their choice of leader. Still, no one had the temerity to arouse Reb Elimelekh.

But when several more hours passed and Reb Elimelekh remained sleeping, they knew they had to do something. They summoned Reb Zusha, who was with them at the inn, to awaken his brother.

"Waking Reb Elimelekh is the simplest thing in the world," he commented, as if he was just asked by the trembling Hasidim to tie a shoe. And with that he entered the room where his brother was sleeping and placed his hand over the mezuza in the room. At that instant Reb Elimelekh jumped out of bed.

The confounded Hasidim asked Reb Zusha to explain what they had just beheld. "As you know," Reb Zusha began, "man must envision the name of God before his eyes at all times. But what is one to do when he slumbers? The answer is that he relies on the ineffable name inscribed in the mezuza.

"Thus, when I covered over the mezuza, my brother no longer had anything to rely on, and was therefore compelled to awake and envision the Almighty before his eyes."

All of the Hasidim released a pent-up, collective sigh of relief. With Reb Elimelekh at the helm, Lizhensk became the Jerusalem of Hasidim.

One of the great hasidic masters, the Divrei Chaim, commented, "Anyone who believes all the hasidic stories is a fool, and anyone who thinks that any of the stories could not have happened is a heretic."

Perhaps we can append this caveat to mean all hasidic stories are true, just not always religious about fact. They are imbued with multiple layers of meanings and implications in the subtle twists and turns of the telling. The stories of the holy brothers, just like the story about the Baal Shem Tov, will transport us back to the magical places of yore, to the peaks of the Galician Carpathians and to the depths of our hearts.

Hanoch Teller
Jerusalem

Preface by the Translator

I am delighted and honored to have a part in bringing this book to the English-reading world.

First because of my deep respect and admiration for my friend and teacher, Simcha Raz, a distinguished Israeli scholar and writer. This is the sixth book I have been privileged to have published in English which was written originally in Hebrew by Simcha Raz. All six books are the product of Simcha Raz's lifelong study of the sacred literature of the Jewish people.

Simcha Raz has the unique ability to gather profound teachings from many places and deposit the sweetness and beauty of Jewish wisdom into a series of outstanding collections on many themes.

I particularly enjoyed translating this collection of tales of the holy brothers Reb Zusha of Anipoli and Reb Elimelekh of Lizhensk. The stories reflect the powerful personalities of two of the best-known hasidic masters, and the deep moral and spiritual heritage which they have bequeathed to future generations. Reb Zusha's exemplary devotion to God and Reb Elimelekh's profound study of Torah and deep connection to the life of a Hasid make them models for the Jewish people of this century.

I want to thank those who assisted in making this translation smooth and accurate: Yocheved Klausner and Sahar Tzur. Yocheved's amazing mastery of both Hebrew and English is a special gift that she shared with me. And Sahar's special knowledge of the art of translating is another amazing gift. Profound thanks to both of them.

I am extremely grateful to my cherished friend, Joshua Landes, a devoted Jew and lover of Hasidism, who encouraged and supported the translation of this special collection. Most appropriately, he has dedicated this book in honor of his beloved mother and sisters.

I am also truly grateful to the Lieberman family of Montreal, Canada, who supported the publication of this book. The Lieberman family are an outstanding example to all in their support for Torah institutions and scholarship, and it is especially meaningful that they have dedicated this book in memory of their grandfather and fathers, all born in Lizhensk.

I am also grateful to Ashirah Yosefah, of Koren Publishers Jerusalem, for guiding my book from manuscript to press, to Aryeh Grossman of Koren Publishers for his valued assistance in enabling this project to become a reality, and to Esther Cameron and Debbie Ismailoff, whose superb editing is deeply appreciated.

In closing I want to thank my devoted wife, Maxine (Miryam), who tolerated my obsession with the computer during our first years after making aliya. Working on editing and translating this amazing book has brought me great joy and renewed appreciation of the Jewish tradition to which we have together devoted our lives.

Rabbi Dov Peretz Elkins
The Holy City of Jerusalem
Rosh Ḥodesh Shevat 5778

Introduction

REB ZUSHA OF ANIPOLI

Reb Zusha (1718–1800), son of Rabbi Eliezer Lipman of Lizhensk, was the essence of piety, simple faith, and pure, genuine love of Jews. He was the authentic symbol of the image of the tzaddik of former times, who had boundless love for his Creator, the Torah, and the Jewish people.

Reb Zusha's learning came second to his deep piety. "Being naive is a sign of great wisdom," said Rabbi Naftali Tzvi of Ropshitz. Our father Yaakov was "a mild man who stayed in camp,"[1] but not out of naïveté. He met challenges with Lavan and with Esau. He was wise in his simplicity, and Reb Zusha, too, was simple out of choice.

In the city of Anipoli, the last city where Rabbi Dov Ber, the great Maggid of Mezritch, lived, Reb Zusha guided the Hasidim and merited to be buried next to the grave of this illustrious leader of the hasidic movement. He served him in life and served him in death.

When Rabbi Shneur Zalman of Liadi published his famous work, the *Tanya,* the foundational book of hasidic philosophy, he did not seek approbations from the great scholars of Israel. The approbations of Reb Zusha and his colleague Rabbi Yehudah Leib HaKohen of Anipoli, author of *Or HaGanuz,* were all he sought.

---

1. Gen. 25:27.

Rabbi Shneur Zalman testified to the godliness of Reb Zusha: "His prayers were filled with extreme awe, so that in the 'Temple of Awe' his awe was amazing." When Reb Zusha lay ill in his last years and was confined to his sickbed, Rabbi Shneur Zalman made a special trip to Anipoli to serve him.

Reb Zusha entered the garden of *Ḥasidut* before his brother Reb Elimelekh. When Reb Elimelekh still opposed the new trend, Reb Zusha was already learning from the Maggid of Mezritch. Zusha worked on his brother, exposing him to all kinds of teachings, lessons, stories, and wise insights, until he brought his mind and heart into the new movement. And thus Elimelekh became a rabbi, rose to the level of master and guide to generations, and established his own beit midrash. He holds a place of honor even today as a spiritual guide to the Hasidism of Poland and Galicia, while the image of Zusha the wanderer persists to this day.

Zusha always remained Zusha – a simple, honest Jew, never touched by a drop of arrogance or egotism. Reb Zusha never created a congregation, never aspired to greatness or glory, to heroism or royalty. He had but one desire: to be Zusha. What benefit would it serve, he taught, were I to exchange places with our father Avraham? Avraham would be Zusha, and what benefit would come to the world?

Reb Zusha was completely wrapped in ecstasy. The kindling oil of enthusiasm never left him for even a moment. His soul longed endlessly for the greatness of God. He was totally at one with the essence of his Creator.

Reb Zusha had no special approach to Torah study, to Hasidism. He had no secret knowledge; he asked few questions. Nor was he a scholar or one who led followers to ways of faith. In his core he was a simple, honest Jew, a hidden tzaddik, who stands in the corner and prays quietly. One hardly notices him or pays him special attention. But by dint of the purity of his prayers, free of any cunning or biases, all the prayers in the beit midrash found their way to Heaven.

Reb Zusha was well known as a symbol of the movement of those who were pious, God-fearing, and pure, who sought nothing for themselves – neither lucre nor glory, not pleasure in this world or the next. He was simply pure. He fitted the definition of the upright delineated by Eliezer Steinman, the great scholar of Hasidism in this generation. Steinman writes:

One who is upright is always upright, totally honest. He is completely upright. No one is more upright than such a one. The upright person needs not a speck of guile. He is pure and innocent. His uprightness is limitless. Thus he is completely fit and honest. He is honest because there are no detours on the ladder toward heaven, and no slipperiness on the slope downwards.

You might say: An upright person has no depth. Not so! He is deeper than the deepest. A deep person must delve rigorously to reach the depths. But the upright one reaches the depths even on the surface. The upright one does not have to be a scholar. He recites "Blessed are You" and has already reached the depths. He takes a piece of chalk in his hand, or a flower, or a crumb of bread, and behold, he has already attained the whole world. The upright one is always able to transmute a little into a lot. The upright one is righteous. The upright one always stands on the edge of the abyss, but holiness protects him; "God protects the upright."

Reb Zusha is that upright person. Others reached great heights, penned holy books, left behind important Torah interpretations, and he is just Reb Zusha. But when one pronounces the name of Reb Zusha, it has a powerfully strong and majestic sound. Reb Zusha's name means something.

The upright person is not the opposite of the scholar. On the contrary, he is an absolute scholar. And he is not a close neighbor to the one "who doesn't know how to ask." With him, he doesn't know how to get angry, or become embittered. In any case the upright one is not gratuitously contentious, he is not one who starts an argument about the order of the universe, or about the nature of creation, or who strives to solve problems and explain riddles. Since he has no arguments, he needs no answers.

The upright one is righteous, in other words, complete. He finds completeness everywhere. With an open heart he is assured in his heart, in his soul, in his blood, in all his limbs, that whatever the Creator made, He made it well and at the proper time. It is obvious that the upright one sees no evil. There is no such thing as evil. Goodness means absolute simplicity, even though it brings nothing new. He is simply good from birth.

The world of the righteous one is an endless song, a thread of grace and harmony covers it completely. This is not a matter of special intelligence, in the realm of wisdom or at the edge of wisdom. The righteous one is complete in his soul, and since completeness and a greeting of peace[2] is in his very bones he shares greetings with everyone. Every morning he says, as does Zusha: "Good morning to you, O world!" Even to the morning itself he says: "Good morning to you, O morning." The soul of the righteous does not break. It comes from the source of the souls which fled before the eating of the Tree of Knowledge, prior to *shevirat hakelim* (the "breaking of the vessels").[3]

REB ELIMELEKH OF LIZHENSK

Reb Elimelekh (1717–1787), also the son of Eliezer Lipman of Lizhensk, was one of the most important leaders of the hasidic movement.

In his youth he took on the burden of exile and accepted great agony and suffering. Under the influence of his brother Reb Zusha, he embraced Hasidism. He visited the Maggid, Rabbi Dov Ber of Mezritch, and became one of his disciples.

Following the death of Rabbi Dov Ber, Reb Elimelekh traveled to Lizhensk and began to spread the light of Hasidism in Galicia and in Poland. As a leader he acquired for himself such a central position in Hasidism that he was compared to the revered Baal Shem Tov (the Besht).

Reb Elimelekh merited, appropriately, the appellation of "founder of practical Hasidism."

In accordance with the needs of the time, Reb Elimelekh equated the practical form of Hasidism with the deep, theoretical philosophy of the Maggid of Mezritch on the subject of the tzaddik and his qualities. The tzaddik, in the view of Reb Elimelekh, is holy at birth, just as an

2. This is a play on words: "*shalem*," meaning whole, complete, and "shalom," the everyday greeting, which means "peace."
3. *Sha'ar HaḤasidut*, Hotzaat Neuman, Tel Aviv, 317.

oldest child is holy from his mother's womb, and he is considered a son of the Blessed Holy One.

Before aligning himself with the hasidic movement, Reb Elimelekh was a kabbalist who practiced asceticism in his life. Despite the fact that one of the characteristics of Hasidism is that it does not reject worldly matters, there are clear indications that Reb Elimelekh continued to cling to his former ideas.

The Baal Shem Tov was the architect of Hasidism. In his shelter Rabbi Yaakov Yosef of Polnoye and Rabbi Dov Ber of Mezritch established their home and the home of their loyal students, but this meeting place for scholars and aspiring tzaddikim became a firm and faithful home only once Reb Elimelekh set in it a table for guests from the class of simple folk. He made Hasidism an inn for the masses, a house for the people. The Baal Shem Tov set up an "Ohel Moed,"[4] his students turned it into a tabernacle, and Reb Elimelekh built a small sanctuary, since it was he who established the table, which was the foundation for the spread of Hasidism and the leadership of the community.

Since Reb Elimelekh gave Hasidism its final form, refined it, and emphasized the importance of the great tzaddik on whom the whole world relies, he made it a useful, sought-after tool for the masses. Some people revered him as much as they revered the Baal Shem Tov, as if the hasidic movement had two *ḥatanei Torah* or two *ḥatanei Bereshit* standing under one *ḥuppa*. However, it is not appropriate to compare souls with weights and measures like things of this world. Every exceptional person is unique.

The Besht occupies a special place of honor. He is almost not in the category of flesh and blood. He is a spark from the world of legend. He is a messenger of divine providence who was sent to the people at a time of turmoil to extricate them from a mire of decadence and depression of the soul. He is a kind of heavenly voice from the soul of the nation, emerging to awaken and encourage. But Reb Elimelekh is not superhuman, nor is he a genius. He is a simple Jew who rose from the simple people to become a leader of the community, and this is the source of his great strength and special merit.

4. The Tent of Meeting in the Bible.

Reb Elimelekh emphasized especially the spiritual exile, since he knew that the Shekhina (Divine Presence) is with us in exile. Thus "one must meditate alone before the sun rises, when it is a favorable hour to weep over the exile of the Shekhina until there are no more tears." It is a clear sign that a person repents "when one weeps over the exile of the Shekhina," since "in this way one will know if he is on the true path in his service of the Blessed One, when he says that he worries and is pained constantly about the exile of the Shekhina and the people of Israel."

Like the rest of the leaders of Hasidism, Reb Elimelekh emphasized the importance of joy in divine service, and along with this he had an essential understanding of the need for a measure of seriousness, which, according to what is written about him, also existed in his life.

Reb Elimelekh's book, *Noam Elimelekh,* published in Lemberg in 1787, quickly became an important guidebook for Hasidim and was reprinted many times. Rabbi Mendel of Rimanov, the great *Admor*[5] of Galicia, said, "Only after my immersion in the *mikve,* on Erev Shabbat, can I plumb the depths of *Noam Elimelekh.*"

Written as a commentary on the Torah, *Noam Elimelekh* contains much material detailing the ideology and way of life of Hasidism. Reb Elimelekh highlights the idea of the tzaddik. He stresses the role of the rebbe as the source of understanding, as a highly evolved human who lives on a lofty plane, and who is the bridge between God and man. In most editions there is a list of *hanhagot* (religious practices) which Hasidim of all streams try to apply.

Noam Elimelekh is one of the most important foundational books of Hasidism, and it became a sacred volume. Many considered this book as a remedy and placed it at the head of those who were ill or giving birth.

As we already mentioned, Reb Elimelekh came to Hasidism not on his own, but rather under the influence of his brother Reb Zusha. Nevertheless, he eventually reached very high levels of understanding of

5. This is the Hebrew acronym for *Adonenu, Morenu, VeRabbenu* (our lord, our teacher, and our master).

Hasidism and became a teacher of its precepts. Even the giants among the rebbes sang the praises of his book, which to this day is considered a major resource, similar to *Toldot Yaakov Yosef*. Since its publication there has not been another book written on the philosophy of Hasidism equal to it. It is filled with the light of redemption, freeing man from the vain pleasures, pain, and sickness of this world. Yet Reb Elimelekh himself, in contrast to the rest of the great scholars of Hasidism, and even in contrast to his brother Reb Zusha, was not redeemed.

Reb Elimelekh of Lizhensk was only seventeen years old at the beginning of the Baal Shem Tov's leadership and about forty when the Baal Shem Tov died. Had he wanted to, he could have established a connection with him lasting many years, until the latter's death. But Reb Elimelekh chose not to do so, because he did not approve of the appellation "Baal Shem (Master of the Name), as magic makers and those who dealt with oaths and holy names – methods that the holy Ari already considered to be dangerous and outdated – were referred to by this title. Only after Reb Elimelekh recognized the holiness and purity of the Baal Shem Tov and it was clear to him that the title Baal Shem had no connection to the Baal Shem Tov did he join his camp. Since at that point the Baal Shem was no longer alive, Reb Elimelekh accepted the authority of his student, Rabbi Dov Ber, and attained an important position among his followers.

Following Reb Elimelekh were his superb students: Rabbi Yisrael of Kozhnitz, who was dubbed "the second Baal Shem Tov"; Rabbi Yaakov Yitzḥak Horowitz, the Seer of Lublin; Rabbi Mendel of Rimanov; and Rabbi Avraham Yehoshua Heschel of Apta. All of these individuals were considered by the Hasidim as the major followers and spiritual heirs of Reb Elimelekh of Lizhensk.

Compared to all the other great teachers of Hasidism, who were men of esoteric knowledge, Reb Elimelekh's teachings were the most open. It is easier for us to grasp his spirit, to identify with his struggles, to dwell in his proximity and hear from him both new insights into Torah and stories about life and its complications.

Just as the Maggid of Mezritch built his hasidic philosophy on the foundation of the ideas of the Besht, so too did Reb Elimelekh design his beit midrash with the concepts that he imbibed from the Baal Shem Tov's teachings. The Maggid was like a father and patron for his students, and so was Reb Elimelekh. They were similar in their ideas, but different in their actions, of one mind in thought, but different in goals and aspirations. The Maggid was a teacher to students, while Reb Elimelekh was a teacher to rebbes. The Maggid taught the philosophy of Hasidism, while Reb Elimelekh was a guide to the hasidic path.

Hasidic literature, whose existence spans two hundred years, is surprising in several ways, not only in its volume. It stands out in the multiplicity of its subject matter and its creativity. It includes volumes of philosophy and ideology, commentaries on the Torah, and expository essays on rabbinic literature. It also includes sermons, homilies, reprimands, discussions and parables, wills, and stories and legends.

Now *The Holy Brothers* joins this growing body of literature. Its objective is to create a window through which the reader can view the essence of his own life, and, in the words of the founder of the hasidic movement, Rabbi Yisrael Baal Shem Tov, "to affix a mezuza on the gates of the universe, to prevent evildoers from entering," and thus to enjoy the words of Torah taken from that treasured tome, *Noam Elimelekh*, and from the many collections of tales reflecting the way of life of these holy brothers, Reb Zusha and Reb Elimelekh, may their merit protect us and the entire nation of Israel forever.

Simcha Raz

Jerusalem, the tenth of Tevet, 5769

(the *yahrtzeit* of my mother, Hannah Malkah Rakover, of the Mandelbaum family, granddaughter of the great sage Rabbi Menahem-Nahum Epstein of Kobryn, may the memory of the righteous be for a blessing)

Awe of Heaven

HIS TEACHING IS IN ORDER

Just as a father holds the hand of his young son to lead him on the way, so Reb Elimelekh grasps the hands of his Hasidim to show them the right path. His well-known "Tzetel Katan" (handbook for serving God) is the embodiment of a *Kitzur Shulhan Arukh* (abbreviated code of Jewish law) for proper behavior, a kind of menu of mitzvot and good deeds to achieve perfection in Hasidism and in piety. It is a scroll of testimony to the special method of teaching to which he was partial.

At the bottom of the "Tzetel Katan" it is written in simple fashion, "These are the things which if one does them he shall live by them." In this small handbook there are no arguments regarding Jewish laws, no kabbalistic meditations on the unity of God, but rather proper advice, clear and brief, regarding one's customs in thought, speech, and action that one should practice in order to keep away from sin and enter the gates of holiness.

First and most important of all is the acceptance of the yoke of the sovereignty of Heaven – to be at all times literally a servant of the Creator, to keep the mitzvot. And it is possible to keep the mitzvot at every single moment.

The Hasidism of Reb Elimelekh was focused completely on deeds. Even from this perspective there still remained with him some remnants of the ideology of the older Hasidism, which preceded the approach of the Baal Shem Tov (the Besht). Reb Elimelekh still did not remove from his heart the idea – more accurately the feeling – that one cannot attain perfection of the soul except through the destruction of the body, and that there is no way for the soul to rise other than through the flame that burns away materiality. However, the furnace of afflictions he directed toward himself alone. In "Tzetel Katan," which is a path for others, there is no mention of an obligation to accept punishments and afflictions, but there is guidance about the use of language, purity of thought, study of Torah, and prayer with sincerity.

Also included are explanations about what one should do to acquire positive character traits: he should not be lazy or irresponsible; he should accustom himself to arise from his bed early, clean his body, and go quickly to the beit midrash; and he should "become habituated for forty consecutive days to pay attention to the words coming from his mouth, both secular words and spiritual words, and he should imagine that someone standing next to him is encouraging him in a loud voice to fulfill all these instructions regarding behavior. And when he accustoms himself thus, then in the course of time there will arise in him a great awakening of his soul, 'sparks of fire in a mighty flame, a very flame of the Lord.'[1] This is because 'every habit becomes a master.'"

Thus we see in all his simple counsels, some of which are very down-to-earth, the sensitive educator in him, along with the correct logic of a physician. Other tzaddikim were occupied with remedies, charms, and invocations, and would teach, caution, and arouse the people with shouts and crying, or with songs and dances. Reb Elimelekh sought to improve the people with medicines. All of his words were healing. But he was careful not to stuff them with sharp, bitter medicines such as those which he himself used. In his booklet of suggested behavior we do not find encouragement for fasting or self-flagellation.

In *Noam Elimelekh* he grants permission to others to serve the Blessed One with all types of service, to bring the material into holiness, and thereby "the Blessed One gives people permission to enjoy a bit of this world." In his commentary on *Parashat Ki Tissa,* on the verse "Take for yourself choice spices … solidified myrrh …,"[2] he writes:

1. Song 8:6.
2. Ex. 30:23.

> A sweet smell will accompany your deeds; namely, that even with regard to the most material things, from all of the materiality there should emit a pleasant smell. This is the meaning of "solidified myrrh,"[3] which means "bitter" – even if there is something whose purpose is all bitter, a sweet smell should come from it. The word "solidified" (in Hebrew *dror,* literally "freedom") means that you should see that there is freedom, that is, freedom from the angel of death, namely from the devil and oppression of Israel by the nations, all of this you should do with regard to all material matters.
>
> Therefore let no one say that it is forbidden to enjoy things of this world, and that since everything is for the sake of God's name, I will separate myself from all matters of the material world, and not eat or drink at all, and I will be an ascetic. One should not say that, but rather one must strengthen oneself little by little to break the strength of our cravings, and to turn the matter around, around and around, until one finds the point of the essential holiness and its root in all material things.

This holy person, this ascetic, was very strict with himself, fasting constantly. But when he came to teach people the paths of Hasidism and holiness and to set before them a table they could sit around, he educated them according to their nature and their path.

At the same time Reb Elimelekh urged caution in relying on one's own perceptions. Heaven forbid that we should judge the divine providence of the all-knowing Creator with the criteria of human consciousness, which is activated involuntarily by the outside influence of the senses and is subject to the natural constraints of knowledge and experience, without taking into consideration whether the spiritual ear wants to absorb it or not. Since the essence of the Unattainable is exalted above all human concepts, we must hold that, faced with the apparent contradiction between knowledge and choice, one must assume free choice on the part of the Creator, and say by way of allegory that divine providence possesses unlimited freedom; its knowledge possesses

3. The Hebrew words *mor* (myrrh) and *mar* (bitter) are similar.

unlimited freedom to act or hide the matters from the field of its vision, as it is written: "I shall certainly keep My face hidden on that day."[4] Let us not forget that it is forbidden to rely for even a short while on our defective and partial power of distinction when facing these contradictory visions. As the Rambam teaches, we resemble a wanderer in the dark of night, when the path is not lighted other than by the glow of lightning, which appears for a short while and is gone. We must not rely on our ideas, but rather on the facts that our Torah transmits to us, as the revelation of the will of the Blessed One.

YOU SHOULD TAKE LEAVE OF MY ZUSHA

Ḥasidism achieved a great victory when two brothers, Rabbi Shmuel Shmelke, the rabbi of Nikolsburg, and Rabbi Pinhas HaLevi Horowitz, the rabbi of Frankfurt, joined the fellowship of Mezritch. In the early days of the movement, at its sunrise, Hasidism was a kind of spiritual power, built on those things that are neither weighed nor measured: clinging to God, the lifting of the soul and the spirit, joy and longing, awe and reverence, love of God and the Jewish people, thrill and wonder.

When these brothers joined the students of the Maggid of Mezritch, they brought with them precious assets of Torah from the house of their father, Rabbi Tzvi Hirsh Horowitz of Chortkov, and from the beit midrash of Rabbi Elijah of Vilna (the Gra): mastery and sharpness, dignity and depth. The joy in the camp of the Hasidim was great. Even the Maggid himself, Rabbi Dov Ber, rejoiced in welcoming them. He turned his face toward the brothers and said, "I have found a house full of candles, candles flickering but not burning. One spark left my beit midrash, fiery sparks flew off from Hasidism, and the candles caught on fire and became a flame."

However, these sons of the pious Rabbi Tzvi Hirsh of Chortkov were not satisfied when they first came to Mezritch. They remembered the beit midrash of the Vilna Gaon, his room and the Gaon himself, his Torah, his study of the *Ḥumash* (the five books of Moses) – and they missed him. "There," they would say, "we really scooped up Torah with our hands from buckets…." In their first days in Mezritch they were

4. Deut. 31:18.

living in an atmosphere of legends woven around a man who remained mysterious, whose hasidic students saw in him majesty, genius, holiness, blessing; and they, the brothers, felt almost nothing. Here was a special spiritual inspiration, a unique style which expressed itself in song, with an emphasis on the sigh, conveyed with enthusiasm – outward signs to which they had not yet adjusted – and they almost decided to return to Vilna. When they entered the Maggid's room in order to take leave of him, he blessed them in parting and said, "It would be worthwhile if you would also take leave of my Zusha."

Back to Zusha, whom they knew. A righteous man, but…. Yes, they remembered that after meeting them for the first time, he came to them and complained that he was ignorant, illiterate, and he wanted them to teach him a chapter of Mishna every day. They complied and began to teach him the first *mishna* of tractate Berakhot: "From what time may one recite the *Shema*?" They would translate and explain to him each word: "*May-ay-matai* (from what time)" "*korin* (may one recite)" "*Keriat Shema* (the recitation of the three paragraphs of the *Shema*)…." Suddenly Zusha lay down on the floor and began to shout in a loud voice, in dismay and dread: "Who said that '*may-ay-matai*' means 'from what time?' Maybe the interpretation of the mishna is not '*may-ay-matai*,' 'from what time' but rather '*may-ayma*,' 'from fear' – from fear of the Almighty one must recite 'Hear O Israel, the Lord is our God, the Lord is one.'" When he said the word "*eḥad*," "one," his soul almost departed….

A GENIUS IN AWE

Rabbi Menahem Mendel of Kotzk used to say: Just as there is a *gaon* (genius) in halakha, so there are *geonim* in character. One of them is Reb Zusha of Anipoli, who was a giant in the laws of love, awe, and modesty.

HIS AWE COMES BEFORE HIS WISDOM

It happened once that Reb Zusha prayed before the Blessed One, and this is what he said:

Alas! My love for You is greater than my fear of You.
Make it happen, Master of the Universe, that I will tremble and fear You
As the angels and seraphs (fiery angels)
When Your holy name comes clearly from their mouth.

He heard the blessed name in his prayers, and great fear came upon him
Because of the fear of his Creator.
Reb Zusha jumped and spread his hands to Heaven in prayer:
Zusha does not want to be afraid like a dog,
he wants to love You like Zusha.
And the Blessed One listened in His great mercy to his voice.

THE POWER OF LOOKING

"He took him outside and said, 'Look toward heaven and count the stars'" (Genesis 15:5).
The Blessed One said to Avraham:
Do not lower yourself to descend from your level to matters of this world,
Only "Look toward heaven," namely, look at the majesty of God.
One can look at the majesty of God especially
When he looks heavenward and sees the stars in their courses.
They shine with their bright light.
And from this, awe will come to man
to understand the majesty of the Blessed One.
This is the meaning of "count the stars."

– Reb Elimelekh of Lizhensk

LET THE INNER PERSON MATCH THE OUTER PERSON

"When you were famished and weary, and he was undeterred by fear of God" (Deuteronomy 25:18).
There are some people who weary themselves much
with service of the Creator
Until they are very tired,
And nevertheless they have no fear of God.

– Reb Zusha of Anipoli

Between Man and His Fellow Man

A PRAYER

Almighty God, place in our hearts the ability to see in every human being
Only positive attributes and not their faults,
And may we all guide one another on the path of righteousness
That is desirable in Your eyes,
And may there never arise in our hearts hatred for anyone, Heaven forbid.
Amen, may it be Your will.

– Reb Elimelekh of Lizhensk

MARITAL HARMONY AND OFFSPRING

A young man of good stock, dependent financially on his wealthy father-in-law, approached Reb Elimelekh of Lizhensk and poured out his heart: his wife had not borne children, despite their being married ten years. Reb Elimelekh did not pay much attention to him.

After a while the young man came again to Reb Elimelekh with his problem, and again he did not receive any reply. However, during a third visit, Reb Elimelekh asked him: "Is there harmony between you and your wife?"

The young man replied: "Thank God, Rabbi, we have a good relationship and live in harmony together. There is no shouting or arguing in our home, Heaven forbid."

Reb Elimelekh replied: "This is excellent, since there is no blessing better than peace between two married partners. Heaven forbid that they should cause trouble for each other. Our sages warned us that a man should always honor his wife more than himself. But if the two of you are constantly in a state of love and harmony, to the point that there is not a second of a pause in the harmony between you, I suspect that this is what is preventing your wonderful wife from becoming pregnant. So here is my advice: Go home and try to interrupt the bonds of love between you for a very short while, and cause her to become a bit angry about something, and then she too will surely get angry at you. After that return and forgive her, in your love for her, and you will find that the Holy Blessed One will help you very quickly."

The young man returned home, and his wife greeted him as usual with great affection, but he gazed at her in anger, showing displeasure with her, and she too became angry at him. Thus they went from angry looks to angry speech, and in a short while they began to quarrel. In his anger he smacked her. Immediately he felt ashamed before God and regretful that he had done more than his rabbi had asked him – having not stopped at arguing but also hitting her. He waited a while until his anger dissipated and began to speak kindly to her and asked forgiveness. Very soon their family harmony returned.

After some time God blessed the woman and she gave birth to a son. The young man went to see Reb Elimelekh and related to him what had happened and said: "I have no words to thank you, dear Rabbi."

But Reb Elimelekh told him: "I only told you what is hinted in our holy Torah regarding our father Yaakov, of blessed memory. As it is written: 'Yaakov was incensed at Rachel.'[1] Why did Yaakov become angry at Rachel over her asking him for children? What transgression did our mother Rachel commit? One should not be blamed for words spoken in pain. Yaakov became angry at Rachel so that the Holy Blessed One should open her womb."

---

1. Gen. 30:2.

REPRIMAND

The wife of Reb Zusha was quarrelsome and nagged him a lot.

It happened once that Reb Zusha said to her: "Our blessed sages taught: 'One who has a shrewish wife will not enter *Gehinom.*' Maybe it's proper for me to go down into *Gehinom,* as long as I won't be near you."

Immediately Reb Zusha's eyes were opened and there appeared before him the gates of *Gehinom,* with all of its horror. Then Reb Zusha said: "Curse me, woman, curse me!"

THE POWER OF TEARS

Reb Zusha's wife urged him daily to give her a bill of divorce. Thus his heart became very heavy.

One night he called to her and said: "Look here!" And he showed her that his pillow was wet from tears. He continued: "In the Talmud it states: 'Whoever divorces his first wife, even the altar starts to cry.' From these tears the pillow became wet. So now what else do you want? Do you still want a bill of divorce?"

From then on she was quiet. And since she was quiet, she became happy. And when she became happy, she became a good wife.

A BELOVED FRIEND

How does one define a friend? What is the true measure of a friend? A true friend is one before whom you are not afraid to reveal yourself. You don't hold back from exposing to him your innermost secrets, the hidden feelings and experiences beneath the nethermost layer of your soul.

The real meaning of the affection between friends, Rabbi Yitzḥak of Vorka taught, we learn from the Torah: Yehuda, the son of our forefather Yaakov, sent a kid with his Adullamite friend to give to the woman and take back the pledge he had left with her as security. The Adullamite was not a simple man. Nevertheless he agreed to humiliate himself, to search the area and to inquire of neighbors in order to find the harlot, only to save the honor of his friend. From this story we learn that a friend who is not willing to embarrass himself publicly to help a friend in dire distress is not a true friend.

And so while still a youth, Reb Elimelekh decreed for himself an important rule regarding his love for the Jewish people. He made a solemn commitment that every Jew in the world would be equal in his eyes to himself, and that he would not feel in his heart any difference, however small, between his love for his children and his love for the rest of the Jewish people.

It happened once that Reb Elimelekh returned to his city after a long, arduous journey to faraway places. He had not seen his home and family, and had not heard a word about what had occurred there for a very long time. When he arrived at the outskirts of his city there raced by him a wagon harnessed to running horses that had left the city in a big hurry. Unintentionally Reb Elimelekh heard a few words of a discussion between two businessmen who were sitting on the wagon. This is what they said:

Eliezer is a gentle, fine lad, a good soul.... It would be a mitzva to make every effort to save his life; it is forbidden to spare any expense... if only the professor will consent to go and see him..."

Reb Elimelekh froze, his heart began pounding, and a cold sweat covered his whole body: Eliezer – is that not his beloved son, Eliezer? Who knows what happened to him? Why is it necessary to save his life? May the Almighty have mercy!

In a flash the wagon disappeared, and he had no idea to whom to turn to explain the matter of the conversation he had heard. Reb Elimelekh adjusted his satchel on his shoulder and ran quickly toward his house, his heart beating quickly from great worry. On the way he met a number of Jews from his city who were standing and also discussing the urgent situation with Eliezer. When he came closer to them he heard that they were speaking about a different Eliezer, the son of Yehezkel the bath attendant. The deep distress that had permeated his insides dissipated a bit, and he felt better.

Immediately Reb Elimelekh grabbed his head with his hands and began to groan to himself with terrible bitterness:

"Oy, Elimelekh, Elimelekh! Why did you wander around the world? What benefit did you achieve by doing this? What is the value of all your work and suffering if you still feel a difference between your Eliezer and Eliezer the son of the bath attendant?"

Then and there Reb Elimelekh turned around and went away again on another long trip.

THE NATURE OF DISPUTES

"What is an example of a dispute for the sake of Heaven? The dispute between Hillel and Shammai. What is an example of one not for the sake of Heaven? The dispute of Korah and all his company" (*Pirkei Avot* 5:17).

Here's the problem: Why does it not say: "The dispute between Korah and Moshe," just as it says: "The dispute between Hillel and Shammai?"

It is to show that some of those involved in controversy are disdainful of the righteous. And who knows how to tell whether their intent is divine, as they claim it is, or to provoke and scorn honest scholars and Torah students?

Here is how one can determine if they are truthful and their intent is for Heaven's sake: Namely, if we see that their group is united as one person, friends in every way, then surely their intention is totally for the sake of Heaven.

For this is the way of those who are fully and honestly righteous, whose souls are bound together in great love and affection, and who love each other more than themselves, and are not jealous of one another. When they see a friend act greatly, their soul rejoices and their heart is lifted and they hope for more greatness, that he should grow and rise more and more.

But if we see parties in a dispute who do not have unity, who only unite for the sake of controversy as one flame of fire, but in other matters their hearts are separated and divided, and no one can stand to see another's greatness, this is the sign that the fire of contention and arguments which burns in their group is nothing but evil of heart and malice, which brought them to be jealous and speak ill of the righteous who truly do God's work.

This is what the Mishna taught: "Which is a dispute that is not for the sake of Heaven? This is the dispute of Korah and his company." This means that there were 250 men, each of whom desired to be the high priest, as Rashi, of blessed memory, explained. And it turns out that among them their hearts were divided and separate. Only against Moshe were all of them united with an evil intention to argue with him.

So this is "Korah and his company" – a hint that the hearts of Korah and his company were separate from each other. But as for the righteous, their hearts are bound together and all their deeds are for the sake of Heaven.

– Reb Elimelekh of Lizhensk

Confession

AND THUS HE WOULD REPROVE

Reb Zusha was known throughout his life as a righteous tzaddik who took special care to honor every human being. And if he met with a sinner and wanted to reprimand him for his sins in order to bring him back to the good path, he did not turn directly to that sinner and transgressor with words of *musar* (Jewish ethics). Rather he would plant himself in the proximity of the one in whom he wished to awaken thoughts of repentance, and begin to reprove himself with these words:

"Zusha, Zusha! How did you fail by succumbing to the *yetzer hara* (evil inclination) and acting in such and such a way which is not according to the letter of the law?" Here Reb Zusha would attribute to himself the transgressions of the man before whom he stood. "Woe is me, Zusha! What will you say before the heavenly court above, when you give a full accounting about your deeds in this world? Repent, Zusha, since the gates of repentance are not shut as long as the pure soul is not removed from your body!"

Reb Zusha would pronounce these words and similar ones with a broken heart and tear-filled eyes. He would repeat them several times until he thought that the words had entered the heart of the sinner standing beside him and aroused him to return in complete repentance.

It happened once that Reb Zusha came to an inn and saw on the forehead of the innkeeper the transgressions of many years. He stood for a while without moving. But when he was standing alone in his room, a sense of panic and numbness descended upon him in the middle of reciting Psalms, and he called out: "Zusha, Zusha, you evil one, what did you do? There is no lie that did not attract you, and no injustice that you did not taste. Zusha, you fool, you idiot, what will be with you?"

So he listed and counted the sins of the innkeeper, each one in order of its commission and time of its occurrence, as if they were his very own sins, and burst out crying.

The innkeeper, who had been quietly following this amazing man, was standing before the door and heard what he said. At first he was seized with fear, but afterward remorse and kindness blazed in his heart, and his soul was awakened toward God.

BEYOND THE LETTER OF THE LAW

Rabbi Kalonymus Kalman Epstein of Kraków, author of *Maor VaShemesh,* whose main teacher was Reb Elimelekh, said that Reb Zusha was accustomed to list the sins of everyone sitting at his table, without specifying their name, speaking as if he were speaking about himself: "Woe to you, Zusha, thus and thus you have done." He would then go on to mention the sins of every person present.

Rabbi Epstein explained: "I felt that he could read the lines on their forehead, just like the famous Rabbi Yitzḥak Luria, of blessed memory. When I saw that it was my turn I pushed down my hat to cover my forehead. He became silent, so I said to myself, first, that it is forbidden for me to interfere with his work, and, second, I was curious to know what he would say about me – so I uncovered my forehead. Immediately he began: 'Woe to you, Zusha, that you are not careful with performing *netilat yadayim* (ritual hand washing) when you awaken.' Then he turned to the person next to me.

"After the meal I went into his room and told him that since he surely had me in mind, I am surprised about what he said. I do not recall that I ever neglected to perform *netilat yadayim* in the morning. He thought for a while and asked: 'What do you do after your afternoon nap?' I replied that there is no halakha requiring one to perform *netilat yadayim* during the daytime.

"'You are right,' he said to me, 'but since you are a Hasid, you should do things beyond the letter of the law. From now on you should be particular about performing this mitzva.'"

TZEDAKA EVEN WITH THE DECEASED

Rabbi Avraham Yehoshua Heschel of Apta relates this story: "It happened once that Reb Zusha stayed overnight with Reb Elimelekh of Lizhensk, and I assigned him a separate house. One evening I came to his house and found him buried in his thoughts and seemingly communicating with his inner soul. Before he became aware of my presence, I heard him thinking aloud and telling himself: 'My soul, you are not suitable for the World to Come.' And he would count every sin and every blemish and take responsibility for them.

"He became more alert and said to himself: 'Nevertheless even though you are not suitable, the Blessed Holy One in His great compassion will grant for you a portion in the World to Come. Our ancient sages taught: "The Blessed Holy One bestows kindness, clothes the naked, visits the sick, and comforts the mourners."[1] All this He does in this world, so how much more could he do by way of *tzedaka* and loving-kindness in the World to Come, since in that place there is no eating or drinking, no sickness and no death? Surely the Blessed Holy One performs *tzedaka* for those who are not fit for the World to Come, and gives them a place there as an act of *tzedaka*.'"

A MIRACLE WITHIN A MIRACLE

Once Reb Elimelekh and his friend sat at a special meal for Rosh Ḥodesh. Two strangers came along and stood in the doorway. Reb Elimelekh said to those at the table: "Have you ever seen naked bodies like these two Jews?"

One of the men at the table asked in wonder: "Are they really naked? They look clothed to me."

Reb Elimelekh said: "Yes, they are naked. I have never seen a Jew so naked of mitzvot as these two. They have no image of God."

1. Sota 14a.

Reb Elimelekh invited these two strangers to sit at the table and said to them: "Now tell us, fellow Jews, who are you and where did you come from?"

The two men replied: "We came to the rabbi to confess before him. We are sinners and evildoers. Therefore we have lost our Godly image."

Reb Elimelekh said to them: "You two must make a confession. Select one of you to recite your crimes. Do not hide anything, and the Blessed One will have compassion on you. The gates of repentance are not locked even to total sinners."

One of them began to talk. "We have come from Zlotshov," he said. "Once we were wealthy. We had excellent standing in our city. We were partners in business. We were also partners in a large house where we lived comfortably.

"In our business we had an accountant who was faithful and honest. He also had a home near us.

"The *yetzer hara* (evil inclination, Satan) came and enticed us to set our eyes on the home of our loyal employee. We asked him to sell it to us and told him that we would pay him a very generous amount. We would buy it to tear down the house and plant in its place a beautiful garden with a bed of lilies and fruit trees.

"The *yetzer hara* has a big appetite. When our employee heard our suggestion he became very angry at us. 'Is it an insignificant matter that you have a large house, that you also set your eyes on a small house which I built with hard work, and you don't own it?' he said.

"We said to him: 'We hope you will listen to our idea and sell us your house. If not, you will regret it. We will fire you, and another person will take your job and do our accounting.'

"He replied: 'I am not a Canaanite slave to you, and I am not a poor man to obey you for your dirty money. I have saved some money from my salary, thank God, and I can live on that for now until the Blessed One brings me another position.

"We fired him, and he looked for a source of income. When he failed, he decided to open a store in his home. He did that and was not successful. In the end the wheel of fortune turned, and he became poor. In his difficulty he cried and pleaded with us to give him his job back, to save his family from the scourge and shame of hunger.

"We agreed on the condition that he sell us his house for a third of its value. He had no choice, so he received the low price and we signed a contract of sale. After the sale he changed his mind and regretted it, and in his anguish he became ill. Not long afterward he passed away.

"When word reached the children of our loyal employee that their father had died, they came from their far-off city to receive their inheritance. They did not know what had happened to their father before his death – that fortune had turned against him and he had lost his small savings, and even his house had been sold to strangers. They were not aware of the situation, and they already began to quarrel over their inheritance.

"One of them said: 'You take all of our father's money, and I'll take the house, since I don't have one.' Another said: 'I don't want the money or the house. I need Father's store, since I don't have a job.' Another said: 'I don't care who needs what. Let's draw lots and we'll see who gets the money, who gets the house, and who gets the store.' In short, one said this and the other said that. They argued among themselves quite a bit. One made this suggestion: 'My advice is that we should go to the two wealthy men for whom our father, of blessed memory, worked as a loyal employee in their business, and they can help reconcile our needs.'

"The other brothers agreed, and so they did. They went and presented their positions, and we said to them: 'Before you argue over the issues of the money, the house, and the store, you should first clarify if your late father left you money, and if the house and the store were his property.'

"When the brothers heard what had happened to their father they were shocked and even lost their temper: 'Is it possible?' they asked. 'What we last heard is that our late father owned his house and a store.' We explained to them: 'You are wrong. You no longer have any rights to your late father's house. The house was sold to us for two hundred rubles.' When they heard this they were furious. 'This is a lie!' they said. 'Would our father, may his memory be for a blessing, sell this house worth six hundred rubles for two hundred?' We showed them the deed of sale. The brothers said: 'We don't accept this deed of sale. We think you forged it, or it was something you forced upon him. We want to take you to a *din Torah* (rabbinic tribunal) before the local rabbi, Rabbi Yeḥiel Mikhal.'

"We went to a *din Torah* and showed the rabbi the deed of sale. Rabbi Yeḥiel Mikhal said to us: 'Why did you come to mock me? I don't see any deed of sale. This is a blank piece of paper.' The rabbi took the deed, tore it in shreds, and threw it in the trash. We left the rabbi's house with a judgment that took from us the house that we had bought with our own money.

"We were friends with a wealthy nobleman who lived in a palace near Zlotshov, and we had heard from him many complaints about the Jews who rented his properties and his windmills, who were not careful to pay their rent on time. Many would avoid paying completely, declare bankruptcy, or pay him off little by little. We went to this nobleman with libelous reports about Rabbi Yeḥiel Mikhal, saying that he was inciting the Jews to rebel against the noblemen and to refuse to pay their debts to their landlords. We also told him that because of the power of the injunction that Rabbi Yeḥiel Mikhal had placed on the Jews to not trespass on the property of their neighbors, there were not many renters for the properties, and without competition the noblemen could not raise the rent.

"When the nobleman heard this he was fuming; he shook his fists, and said: 'I will teach your rabbi a lesson. I will rip him apart like a fish, I will trample on him like a worm, I will crush him....'

"After a while two armed horsemen arrived at the rabbi's house and ordered him, in the name of the nobleman, to come to the palace to the feast that had been arranged in honor of some important officials. The rabbi's friends understood immediately that serious trouble was in store. Everyone in the city, old and young, went, and with them went Rabbi Yeḥiel Mikhal, weeping bitterly, to the house of authority, the place of evil and cruel people.

"Near the gate of the palace stood armed soldiers who did not permit anyone from the community to enter. The soldiers took the rabbi and brought him with swords in their hands, to the accompaniment of musical instruments, into the palace. The Jews stood outside and wept aloud while the music played. The whole community shook from fear lest they cut off the rabbi's head, Heaven forbid.

"The scheming nobleman planned to do just that, but the Blessed One canceled his evil plan. All the enemies of Israel were embarrassed about coming to the palace to witness the disgraceful death of the holy Rabbi Yeḥiel Mikhal, and they hid their faces. Their shame melted their hearts. The hands of the soldiers holding the swords over the head of Rabbi Yeḥiel Mikhal froze. The musicians stood like robots and could not move their hands. The holy tzaddik Rabbi Yeḥiel Mikhal asked the wicked nobleman innocently: 'What is my crime, and what is my sin against you, that you have brought me here to kill me?'

"The nobleman cried and pleaded before him, saying: 'I see that you are a holy man.... Forgive me, pardon me, Rabbi. Have mercy on me and do not take revenge on me for this.'

"Rabbi Yeḥiel Mikhal forgave him, on condition that in all areas under his control he should give orders not to harass any Jewish renters who could not afford to pay the rent on time. The nobleman agreed and even offered to punish those who had maligned a holy man. But the tzaddik Rabbi Yeḥiel Mikhal ordered that they not be hurt, since judgment belongs to the Blessed God."

The man telling the story concluded: "It is true that the nobleman did not punish us, but the Blessed One repaid us and turned us into paupers. We lost all of our money in a bad deal, and even our house was taken from us by our debtors. We have become beggars who wander from city to city, going from house to house for alms. But we are not mourning over the destruction of our home, rather on the bitterness that plagues us.

"Reb Elimelekh," the two cried in a sorrowful wail, "the holy tzaddik Rabbi Yeḥiel Mikhal has already gone to Heaven, and we are seeking from you repair for our souls."

Reb Elimelekh said to them: "True, your thoughts were evil, but the Blessed One turned it to good, since the heavenly name has been sanctified through you, and the Jewish renters found respite and salvation. With this your sin is pardoned. Now you can go, when your time comes, to stand before the court on high."

In less than a month the two Jews died.

Rabbi Moshe of Lvov told this story to another who came to get *shmura matza* to bring to Rabbi Natan David of Shidlovitz, since it was the custom of Rabbi Moshe to send *shmura matza* every year to Rabbi Natan David. On delivering the matza, the messenger told this story to Rabbi Natan David.

When Rabbi Natan David heard this story from the messenger, he said: "This is indeed a miracle within a miracle. The messenger told the amazing story exactly in the same words, and with the same emphasis and intent, which were conveyed from the mouth of Rabbi Moshe. The tzaddik, the holy Rabbi Moshe, pointed his hands and modulated his voice with the intention of impressing it on the mind of the messenger, and the messenger was able to grasp the exact events just as the two penitents told them."

A HEALTHY BODY AND DIVINE LIGHT

It happened once that a *baal teshuva* (repentant Jew) came to Reb Elimelekh with a slip of paper from one of the great masters, who had decreed upon him several afflictions, fasts, and mortifications. The man had already become frail and weak from some of the afflictions that he had begun to carry out The rabbi told him, "Do not do any of these afflictions, and your heart can be certain that you will not leave here until you do complete repentance."

The rabbi called his son, Rabbi Elazar, and told him, "I am giving you this man to supervise his eating and drinking until he is healthy and strong. When he has regained his strength, bring him to me."

Rabbi Elazar did as his holy father ordered him. When the man had returned to his normal strength, he brought him to his father. The rabbi began to speak to him about the disgrace of the sins, the seriousness of the failure which he inflicted on his soul when he transgressed the order of the King and rebelled against the Lord, until the man felt very guilty and began wailing loudly. Then the rabbi said to him: "My son! Now you must recite the confession. Say *Ashamnu* (we have sinned).'"

The man said *Ashamnu* and immediately fainted upon realizing the greatness of his sin. The people around him hastily aroused him, and the rabbi said to him, "Now go and rest, and when you feel better come back to me again, only do not afflict or punish yourself, Heaven forbid."

After a few days he returned to the rabbi, who again began to speak to him about the disgrace of his sins. This time he ordered him to say *Bagadnu* (we have betrayed). The man said *Bagadnu* and fainted again from the terrible bitterness in his heart.

The rabbi did the same thing again and again. Each time he recited with him just one word of the confession, until he completed it.

Only then did he order him to go home in peace, and the man became a complete *baal teshuva.*

HIS SOUL DEPARTED IN PURITY

A simple man who lived in Jerusalem was on his deathbed, suffering terrible pain, and could not die. When people came to visit him he asked only that they pray to God to take his soul so that he would not suffer any more terrible pain. He would approach death and then improve, approach death and improve, again and again.

Among his visitors was one man who asked him to relate all the events of his life from his youth to the present. The sick man did not remember much, but while talking he related that he had once been in the city of Lizhensk. When the sick man mentioned this, a thought flashed through the visitor's mind. He asked the dying man if he had visited the grave of Reb Elimelekh of Lizhensk.

The sick man replied in wonder, "Is it possible to be in Lizhensk and not prostrate yourself on the grave of that tzaddik?"

"If so," said the man, "the answer is clear. Reb Elimelekh wrote in his will that whoever visits his grave is assured that he will not die without doing *teshuva* (repenting). Therefore, this is my advice to you: recite the confession and do *teshuva.*"

The sick man did *teshuva,* and immediately he died.

HE RETURNED HIS SOUL TO HIS CREATOR

The community workers of the *ḥevra kadisha* (burial society) in the city of Lizhensk were simple men. When it came time for Reb Elimelekh to die, he summoned the members of the *ḥevra kadisha.*

As was their custom, they came and said to him, "Rabbi, confess your sins."

Reb Elimelekh broke down crying: "Where were you all this time when I was sitting at my table eating hearty meals? Then I had the strength to repent and confess my sins. Now I have no strength left."

Reb Elimelekh began to enumerate his "sins," but the only sins he mentioned were those of the people surrounding him.. He listed the sins with honest tears until they all had a spiritual awakening and became true *baalei teshuva.*

Thus Reb Elimelekh returned his soul to his Creator.

Dance and Joy

GO AND ASK ZUSHA

Rabbi Pinhas HaLevi Horowitz, the rabbi of Frankfurt, and his brother Rabbi Shmuel Shmelke, the rabbi of Nikolsburg, were the first to serve as rabbis and court judges in European countries while carrying the banner of Besht-style Hasidism. And despite their Hasidism, the leaders of the *mitnagdim* (opponents of Hasidism) related to them with love and honor.

These brothers, sons of the hasidic Rabbi Tzvi Hirsh of Chortkov, had found the proper and true path in Torah study in the beit midrash of the Vilna Gaon. But in that beit midrash, which was the center of opposition to Hasidism, they had heard about the Maggid of Mezritch and his students and their hasidic ways. From time to time they heard whispers about that "sect" and its approach to the divine, and they became very upset.

They heard that whereas the Vilna Gaon interpreted "His glory" in the verse "the whole world is filled with His glory"[1] as meaning "His providence," Besht-style Hasidism interpreted the verse in its plain meaning: the world is actually filled with His glory, since divinity is in everything, "filling all the worlds." Everything you see and hear, feel and sense, think and observe, everything is divine. In every motion, everywhere you turn, in every thought, in every image and vision, in every storm and in every state of calm, in every sound and in every stillness,

1. Is. 6:3.

in the high mountain and in the grain of sand, in the giant and in the moth, in the most concrete matters and in the most ethereal spirituality – in everything you will find divinity. Thus the Besht would say: "'God of the world' – this teaches you that God's point of view is the point of view of the world, and the point of view of the world is 'the point of view of God. This is the *alef* and the *tav* (A to Z) of Hasidism, and 'the rest is commentary; go and learn.'"

The Horowitz brothers heard these deep ideas, and their souls were thirsty to learn.

Quietly and secretly, according to hasidic legend, they would hide inside the beit midrash of the Vilna Gaon, and together with a few members of the "sect" would enter into the inner chambers in a hasidic *minyan* (prayer quorum) in one of the dark alleys in Vilna. There they would hear from time to time about the divine spiritual joy which Hasidism brought to the service of God, the same joy which in its deep insides, in its root of roots, is also divine sadness, pathos, intense yearning, a longing for that which is beyond the reach of any scholar, *gaon* or holy man.

Their soul craved for this joy, this sadness and this longing.

They remembered the words of the Mishna, "One must bless on evil tidings just as one blesses on good tidings,"[2] and after that the words of the Gemara, "The Mishna's statement was only necessary to instruct us to accept bad tidings with the same joy with which we accept good tidings."[3]

The brothers reflected on the matter, wondering: Hasidism commands joy. The ancient sages require us to accept evil tidings, not only in love but with joy... but how is it possible for a human being, for one of flesh and blood, to bless on evil tidings, and with joy, just as one blesses on good tidings? Perhaps, they thought, they might find an answer to this question in Hasidism.

So they left Vilna and traveled to Mezritch and came to the room of the Maggid, Rabbi Dov Ber of Mezritch. Immediately after the greeting, they presented to him this question. The Maggid said to them, "A simple question like this even my Zusha can answer. Go ask him."

2. Berakhot 54a.
3. Ibid. 60b.

The brothers looked at each other in surprise at this reply. They entered the beit midrash of the Maggid and asked: "Who is this Zusha?" In answer, one of the group pointed to a poor wretch who was standing near the oven, dancing and frolicking and reading the book of Psalms with lyrical emotion, his face glowing with joy.

And that was Reb Zusha of Anipoli.

They approached him and told him that the Maggid had sent them to him, and they put their question to him.

"I am surprised," answered Reb Zusha innocently, "that our holy rabbi sent you to me. This question should be asked of one who has undergone punishment, to one who has experienced some bad times in his life. A person like that may know if it is possible to accept bad things in joy and to make a blessing on them. Zusha never experienced bad things in his life. Zusha has only had goodness and kindness his whole life, and he always blesses for goodness."

The brothers Rabbi Shmuel Shmelke and Rabbi Pinhas heard this innocent answer from one of the hasidic students of the Maggid. He and they became his foremost disciples and followers.

THE MERIT OF DANCING WILL TESTIFY FOR US

It happened once on the day before Shabbat that a villager came to see Reb Elimelekh of Lizhensk and poured out his heart to him: he had a grown daughter and no dowry to marry her off. Reb Elimelekh ordered to have her brought to him immediately. He arranged a marriage for her with the son of a water carrier in the city, gave her a dowry, and made her a wedding. The Maggid of Kozhnitz played the fiddle and the rabbi of Lublin was the merrymaker, and many guests came and danced all during Shabbat evening.

Reb Elimelekh said to his guest Rabbi Shmuel of Korov, who was at the same wedding: "Look at the fire burning around us here." Reb Elimelekh danced with them and said that the Hebrew words *ḥesed* (kindness) and *emet* (truth) have the same *gematria* (numerical value) as *ḥatan* (bridegroom) and *kalla* (bride).

Later he said: "Master of the Universe, as payment for the mitzva of dancing which we have performed, may we merit at least to extinguish one ember which is prepared for us in *Gehinom*."

THE JOY OF A MITZVA

A wedding procession once passed near the home of Reb Zusha. Reb Zusha saw the procession from his window, went out of his house, and danced with great joy in the street before the bride and groom.

When he returned home, his family commented to him that what he did was not proper, and that it was beneath a man of his stature to go out and dance in the street for some passing wedding.

Reb Zusha replied: "I will tell you a story.

"When I was a young student of the holy Rabbi Yeḥiel Mikhal, the Maggid of Zlotshov, of blessed memory, he reproached me once. Afterward he appeased me and said, 'Reb Zusha, forgive me for humiliating you.'

"I replied: 'My master, I forgive you.'

"Before I went to sleep he came to me again and said again, 'Reb Zusha, forgive me.' And I answered again. 'I forgive you, my master.'

"After I had gone to sleep, the father of my rabbi, the holy Rabbi Yitzḥak of Dorohovitch, of blessed memory, appeared to me from the Upper World and and said to me, 'One son I left in the lower world, and a dear son like that you want to destroy because he insulted you?'

"I answered him, 'Rabbi, I have already forgiven him with all my heart and soul, so what else can I do?'

"He said to me: 'This is still not total forgiveness. Please come with me, and I will show you how to forgive.'

"I got up from my bed and went with him to the *mikve*. There Rabbi Yitzḥak of Dorohovitch, of blessed memory, ordered me to immerse three times in the *mikve*, and each time I should say that I forgive his son.

"I did as he said and came out of the *mikve*. Then I saw that the face of Rabbi Yitzḥak shone with a very great light, so that it was impossible to look at him. I asked him to explain, and he said to me that he merited rays of light because he was careful his whole life regarding the three things that Rabbi Nehuniah ben Hakaneh said caused him to merit a long life: 'In all my days I never attained honor at the expense of a friend's degradation. Nor did my friend's curse ever remain with me at bedtime. And I was always generous with my money.'[4]

---

4. Megilla 28a.

"Rabbi Yitzḥak went on to tell me that what he achieved through these three things, it is possible to achieve by means of joy.

"Therefore," concluded Reb Zusha to his family, "when I saw the joy of the wedding in the street near my home I rushed outside to participate in the joy of the mitzva."

I WILL JOIN THEM

Many Hasidim accompanied Reb Elimelekh when he left Pshevorsk. During the move the enthusiastic Hasidim let the horses loose and harnessed themselves in their place.

Reb Elimelekh got off his wagon and joined the crowd. The people were surprised, and asked: "Why are you doing this?" He answered: "I saw the enthusiasm of a mitzva, and I said to myself: I too will join them."

Exile

"AND MOSHE WENT UP TO GOD"[1]

"When Moshe went up to heaven, the angels said to the Holy Blessed One: Master of the Universe, what is one born of woman doing among us?"[2]

Once during Reb Zusha and Reb Elimelekh's travels to far-off communities, they came to a small town, went into the beit midrash, and sat down to hear the rabbi's discourse.

Several days passed, and during all this time not one person approached them to offer a blessing, say hello, or ask them anything about who they were or where they came from.

Only on the evening of Shabbat, after prayers, when they came to divide the out-of-town guests among the householders for the meal, did the rabbi approach them and ask who they were.

Reb Elimelekh turned to the rabbi and said, "When Moshe went up the mountain to receive the Torah, the angels asked, 'What is one born of woman doing among us? Who is he?'

"Compare this to the time when the angels came to our father Avraham. He did not ask them who they were, since 'one does not inquire whether one is hungry or not – just offer him food.'

1. Ex. 19:3.
2. Shabbat 88b.

"With you, rabbi, we see that it is the opposite. During the study hour no one asked us who we are, and no one even offered a greeting. And only when it came time to eat, to honor us with a meal, you asked and inquired."

THE HEIR

Rabbi Eliezer Lipman, the father of Reb Elimelekh and Reb Zusha and their brothers, was a wealthy villager. When he died, the brothers divided up his inheritance. Rabbi Avraham, the eldest, received the cash. The fields and the houses went to Rabbi Natan. The jewelry and furniture were passed down to Reb Elimelekh. And Reb Zusha inherited all the money due their father from his debtors.

Reb Zusha paid no attention to the whole matter of the inheritance and did not bother to collect the debts, but traveled from city to city to visit many communities.

During his travels he arrived at Mezritch. There he became close to the Maggid, Rabbi Dov Ber, and learned from him the concept of *bittul hayesh* (the negation of existence). From then on he would go from city to city as a pauper in torn clothing, preaching about Hasidism.

His brothers were too embarrassed to have him stay in their home. So they had him stay in the home of a baker, who fed him at his table. But since Reb Zusha's custom was to study and pray at night in a loud voice with great enthusiasm, he disturbed the sleep of the baker and his family. The baker removed him from his house and sent him to the house of Reb Elimelekh.

After the death of their teacher, the Maggid of Mezritch, the two brothers returned to Galicia, the region of their birth. They wandered from village to village and mingled with the peasants there, staying in poorhouses and suffering distress, shame, and insults, sometimes even physical attacks. But little by little they succeeded in imbuing some of the masses, and even some of the Torah students, with the majesty of Hasidism and with true awe of God. According to one hasidic tradition, the two brothers in their wandering even accepted *tikkun hagalut* (nullifying the exile). This was a practice of many kabbalists, including the Gaon of Vilna. For this purpose they would go in rags like beggars, with their bags on their shoulders and a staff in their hands. On the way they studied Torah, both the revealed and the hidden Torah, but it was all done in secret. No one knew their names, and no one recognized them.

MITZVA ACCORDING TO HALAKHA

Once in their wanderings Reb Elimelekh and Reb Zusha came to an inn whose Jewish owner was considered an outstanding host. As soon as the owner recognized that the Blessed Holy One had sent him guests, he prepared a special feast. However, the custom of these holy guests was not to eat during their wanderings, but rather to quiet their appetite and fuel their soul. At this inn they barely touched any food or drink.

The next time they came to this inn, the owner did not permit them to cross the threshold. They said to him: "You are known as a gracious host. Please bring us in and we shall require nothing further of you."

The owner replied, "That is the reason why I do not want to accommodate you. Twice the mitzva of *hakhnasat orhim* (hospitality) is found in the Torah, with Avraham and with Lot. With Lot it is written, 'The two angels arrived in Sodom in the evening.'[3] Lot wanted to bring the angels into his house, since hosting angels in one's house is an honor and costs nothing, as angels do not eat. But with Avraham the angels had to masquerade as humans, as it is written: 'He saw three men standing near him.'[4] Since they saw Avraham fleeing from the Shekhina (Divine Presence) to welcome the guests, they understood that Avraham sought guests, that is, humans who need food, for regarding angels, the Shekhina's glory fills the earth, and it is always possible to greet her."

COLD AND HEAT

During his days of self-imposed exile, Reb Zusha once came to Austria during the festival of Sukkot. Since he was wearing clothes of a downtrodden beggar, no one invited him for the festive meal. The chief rabbi had pity on him and invited him to his home. When the rabbi asked his name, he said, "My name is little Zusha."

3. Gen. 19:1.
4. Ibid. 18:2.

After the meal the rabbi lay on his bed in the sukka, covered with a heavy blanket, while Zusha lay on the ground without a pillow or blanket, either because he refused to lie comfortably, or because even the rabbi was not careful to fulfill the mitzva of hospitality properly for a poor beggar.

During the night Zusha suffered from the cold night air, and he began to mumble in his sleep: "Oy, Zusha is cold. Wicked Zusha is not accustomed to enjoy the mitzva of dwelling in the sukka."

While Zusha was mumbling, the sukka suddenly became unbearably warm. The local rabbi was obliged to remove his heavy blanket, and yet he was still warm.

Zusha said: "Oy, it is too hot in the sukka. It is a pity for the rabbi to have to languish in the heat."

While Reb Zusha was still speaking, the heat in the sukka vanished, and in its place came a very cold wind. Again the rabbi wrapped himself in his blanket. Then the heat returned. And so the same event occurred several times.

The next day, the rabbi extended great honor to his beggar guest, and no longer called him "little Zusha" but rather "the great Reb Zusha."

Reb Zusha said: "As long as Zusha is Zusha, he is little Zusha. But when he is called Reb Zusha, and even the great Zusha, Zusha is no longer…."

FLOGGING

Elimelekh and Zusha expected to be attacked occasionally during their wanderings. In those days it was the rule that a wanderer would receive blows to his body. The main point of these long journeys, when they would wander from city to city, visiting inns and taverns as well as *batei midrash,* was to endure a fair share of attacks.

One who is full of himself has no room for anything else, but one who is empty becomes a vessel for the abundance of the Supreme Being. The only way to achieve this is to dress in the clothing of the poor, to take one's staff and satchel and go from house to house in faraway places, to visit inns and taverns, where, whenever something is lost or stolen, they blame the beggar. It is assumed that a beggar is a thief or a thug, even when there is no one to mock or curse him and to make a joke at his expense by flogging him to the laughter of the crowd.

And so it happened that on one of their self-imposed exiles, Reb Elimelekh and Reb Zusha came to spend the night at a certain inn where there was a wedding. The two brothers sat on the side as poor guests, dirty and untidy. Among the wedding guests were a few fellows, who, when they had too much to drink, became rowdy and grabbed the poor man sitting at the end of the table. Between the dances they put him on the floor and threw some punches at him. When the dancing started again they let him be until the next break, when they unfortunately returned. Dancing and punching made the crowd hysterical.

As fate would have it, the poor man at the end of the table was Reb Zusha. Fate always wants – if in fact it knows what it wants – the good juicy piece. It wanted Zusha to be complete and whole.

Reb Elimelekh, on the other hand, sat pensively near the wall on his bag, feeling jealous of his brother Zusha, who was lucky enough to absorb the punches, and wondering why he was deprived.

While the hooligans were dancing wildly, he stood and chatted quietly with his brother, asking him to switch places since Zusha had already received punches twice. So they changed places when the dancers were not looking, so that they would not get the nasty idea of pulling Zusha from his corner after they had degraded him and accustomed him to their punching.

The dance ended, and as luck would have it, a feeling of decency was aroused in one of the thugs, and he said: "Why are we wasting all our punches on this fool sitting at the end of the table and restraining our hand from this guy in the corner? Let's honor him with an ample supply, and give some rest to the weary bones of this one." They dragged the one from the corner – obviously again Zusha – and began to slap him on the back all over again, to give the second idler a taste of some good smacks.

"Look, my beloved brother," Reb Zusha explained to his brother, "the smacks come to the person whom fortune chooses. Sit where he will, they will reach him in his place, and he will not be deprived of his share.

"Zusha, the last to be honored, will always be the first to be beaten."

THE END OF WANDERING

The sacred commitment of Reb Elimelekh was to be a wanderer, just like other poor people who go from door to door. He would ask God: When will I no longer have to be a wanderer? The answer then came: when a man and a woman beat him, this would be the sign that the end of the exile has arrived.

It happened that he came to a city where they gave him a Shabbat meal in the home of a worker. The wife said to him, "Whenever you eat with us you will do some work for me to help prepare for the holy Shabbat." "What kind of work?" he asked. "To chop some chips of wood," she answered.

Reb Elimelekh took the axe to chop the wood. He was a very tall man, and the room had a low ceiling. When he raised the axe in a hurry he accidentally hit the copper lamp that hung from the ceiling, and the lamp broke. When the owners saw that the poor man had broken the lamp, they pounced on him and beat him with vigorous blows.

That very Shabbat many of the local citizens came to him and called him "Rabbi."

WHO AM I, AND WHAT AM I?

For five consecutive years Reb Elimelekh and Reb Zusha wandered from city to city and from village to village and suffered hunger, insults, and whippings. Finally they decided they had had enough of wandering and would seek permanent places to live and would spread the philosophy of Hasidism in their local city.

At that time they came to Liska, where the chief rabbi was Rabbi Menahem Mendel Horwitz, a giant in Torah and well born. It was the custom of the two brothers during their wanderings to distance themselves from the wealthy and privileged, and even from outstanding scholars and famous rabbis, since whenever one gets close to a great person, whether in wealth, in Torah, or in aristocracy, then he too becomes great in his own eyes and is drawn to arrogance. This is what happens when one entertains arrogant thoughts, which crawl like a worm into the inner soul and devour the divine energy.

Therefore in every town the brothers came to, they would seek out only simple Jews, the poor and the needy, the lowest of the low, wagon drivers and servants; they would sleep in the poorhouse, in the beit midrash behind the stove, or in the house of some poor *melamed* (teacher) or water carrier.

But in Liska, since they had already decided to end their wandering and even to stop being self-effacing and to spread Hasidism in a public way, they wanted to approach the community rabbi, who was outstanding in Torah and fear of Heaven. They hoped to get his blessing and even to hear some words of Torah from him.

They came to the rabbi, stood in the doorway before him, and asked for a donation. The rabbi gave them a knowing glance, and said to them in a pleasant way, "*Shalom aleikhem,* my friends." Then he gave each of them a coin and said nothing further.

When they left the house, each saw a gold dinar in his hand. Reb Elimelekh said, "Elimelekh is afraid to keep the gold dinar, lest the rabbi made a mistake and intended to give a copper coin. Elimelekh nevertheless had pleasure from the thievery."

Reb Zusha said, "Zusha is afraid to keep the gold dinar, lest the rabbi of Liska mistakenly thought that the two poor men were scholars, and Zusha deceived the rabbi and is a thief."

Reb Elimelekh said, "Zusha, my brother, therefore there is no doubt. You are surely a scholar. But Elimelekh is evil and arrogant. And now that he has been given a gold coin, it is obvious that he will become arrogant and will say: This is the power of Elimelekh, that even though he is dressed like a beggar and puts out his hand, he puts a gold coin in his pocket, as is the custom of a scholar, and surely the Shekhina envelops him."

Reb Zusha said, "Heaven forbid, Elimelekh, that you put a stain on your holy soul, and say that you are arrogant. There is certainly an error here. The gold dinars are not ours. Come, my brother, and we shall return them to the rabbi of Liska."

They returned to the house of the rabbi and told him that they had come to return the stolen goods, since one does not give a gold dinar to a beggar. They said that it seemed that the rabbi of Liska had made a mistake and exchanged a gold coin for a copper coin.

The rabbi of Liska said to them, "No, my masters, there is no mistake. No copper coin was exchanged for a gold coin. Thank God I have good intuition. I recognized that you were worthy of a decent amount." Again he gave them a penetrating glance. "But it seems to me that Jews who wander for five consecutive years should reach a level of total nonentity, to the point of real submission, without an ounce of selfishness, so as to be truly righteous and to receive in love not only punishment, but also a bit of pleasure."

When they heard this, they accepted upon themselves an additional year of wandering.

I REMAINED THE WAY I WAS

It was the custom of the two brothers during their days of wandering that when they came to a city or a town they would stay with one of the teachers who they knew to be a kosher, God-fearing Jew. After their years of wandering came to an end, and Reb Elimelekh settled in the city of Lizhensk, he made his living as one of the leading hasidic masters. From near and far students came to him to seek Torah or a blessing from him.

It happened once that he was asked by the community leaders of a town in Galicia to honor them with a visit. He had passed through this town more than once, together with his brother Reb Zusha, and they had always stayed with one of the teachers who leaned toward Hasidism. Now Reb Elimelekh acceded to the request of the community leaders and traveled to the town in a horse-drawn carriage.

One of the prosperous Hasidim in the town came to greet him and requested that he honor him by staying at his home. Reb Elimelekh did not promise anything, but suggested that he return to the town and he would follow him. When Reb Elimelekh came to the town he returned again to the same teacher who had hosted him in his wandering days.

The wealthy Hasid heard about this and was very upset. He came to Reb Elimelekh and began to complain: "Rabbi, I have exerted so much effort. I cleared out the best room in the house for you, I prepared a sumptuous feast for the Hasidim, so why not give me the privilege, holy rabbi, of fulfilling the great mitzva of *hakhnasat orḥim* for one as important as you?"

Reb Elimelekh answered with deep humility and a lowly spirit: "I do not know what special quality you found in me now that you want to honor me and host me in your house. Previously, when I would wander from place to place, and even now, I don't see in myself even one special quality in which I can take pride. I have not changed for the better, and it is proper that I not change my place of lodging.

"However," added Reb Elimelekh after some light-hearted thought, with a smile on his face, "you want to honor me now, because you found in me a change for the better. Before now I would wander on foot from place to place, and now I have come here in a horse-drawn carriage. So take the carriage and the horses, and bring them into your house, and fulfill thereby the mitzva of *hakhnasat orḥim*."

BREAD TO EAT AND CLOTHING TO WEAR

Once Reb Zusha came to the large city of Ostroh. Since his reputation was already widely known, the people of the city came out to greet him with much honor and glory and prepared a special feast for him and all the local citizens.

During the meal, while sitting at the head of the table with all the important people of the city around him, Reb Zusha began to take the dishes off the table. He placed them on the silk coat that he was wearing and called out:

"Take, silk coat. Eat and fill yourself! It is in your honor that this whole feast was prepared."

And turning to the astonished people, he explained: "Many years ago I lived with my family for a while in your city, in a damp cellar under a certain building on a certain street. The poverty in my house was very difficult, and there were days in which there was not even one meal to feed the children. Even though it says in the Talmud: 'They do not examine the level of poverty of one who asks for food,'[5] there was no one who took pity on our poor family to give us even a piece of salty bread and a cup of water.

"I am now sitting and examining my soul: What has changed from then to now? Then there was no one who thought to give Zusha a piece of dry bread, and now I am served a lavish meal – but Zusha has not changed one iota from then to now! I have come to the conclusion, therefore, that the feast is meant for the silk coat that I am wearing, because that alone is the difference between what I was then and what I am now!"

---

5. Bava Batra 9a.

TO FEEL THE FEELING

It happened once that the followers of Rabbi Yitzḥak of Neschiz asked their teacher: "Why did Reb Elimelekh and Reb Zusha take so many long journeys? If they wanted to mortify themselves, they could have done it in their homes."

The rabbi replied: "To feel the pain one must taste it, like food."

Hospitality

THE SICK MAN'S BLESSING

The father of Reb Elimelekh and Reb Zusha lived in a village near a tavern and was known for his hospitality.

Once a large group of beggars came there. The master of the house and his wife received them graciously and gave them food and drink and a place to sleep. The beggars asked them to heat up the bathwater so that they could bathe, and the hosts complied with their request.

There was among them a poor man who was suffering from boils that covered him from head to toe, and none of the beggars wanted to bathe with him. The mistress of the house had compassion on him and bathed him. The afflicted man said to her, "As a reward for this I shall bless you that you will give birth to sons like me."

The woman was very troubled by his words: Children with boils....

When he had finished speaking, the wagon and the beggars, including the sick man, disappeared. The couple understood that this had been a test from God, to bring them the merit of having holy sons.

When the elderly master, the Baal HaTanya, Rabbi Shneur Zalman of Liadi, told this story, one of his listeners asked him, "Who was that sick man?"

The Baal HaTanya held his tongue and did not answer.

I GRANT MERIT TO THE MASSES

On one of his wandering trips, Reb Zusha of Anipoli went into synagogue on Sabbath eve to recite the *Kabbalat Shabbat* prayers. Because he was dressed shabbily as a lowly beggar, people were suspicious of having him in their home, and no one invited him for the Sabbath meal. Finally the *shamash* of the synagogue had pity on him and invited him to enjoy the Sabbath meal at his home.

All of a sudden, in the midst of the meal, Reb Zusha began to express his joy in loud laughter, and since he was in such a good-humored mood he began to kiss his own hands.

Seeing these antics, the host family looked at him with fear and suspicion. Reb Zusha understood that they thought he had lost his mind. He said to them: "You may relax, good people. Zusha is not completely crazy. But Zusha is truly happy to be sitting at a table of kosher Jews, who merited to fulfill the mitzva of *hakhnasat orḥim* through me. Therefore Zusha is happy that he resembles an etrog. Do people stare at the etrog all year long? All year the etrog is a foolish fruit, so when does it rise to greatness? On the festival of Sukkot, when the Blessed Holy One commanded us to perform the mitzva with this etrog. So too, Zusha is always a foolish fruit, who merits that a mitzva be performed through him.

"Therefore Zusha now loves Zusha – who now resembles an etrog."

THE GUEST AND THE HOST

Reb Elimelekh was one of the righteous men of his generation. However, for a long time before his name became known among the masses, his friends did not know if he was counted among the Ḥasidim, even though he already conducted himself as such clandestinely. So when the time came for him to reveal himself, it was as difficult for him as the parting of the Reed Sea, since he did not see himself in this way.

What did he do? He accepted upon himself the yoke of exile, wandering from city to city and from village to village. At the outset he pledged not to stay in any one place more than twenty-four hours. Since he had inflicted on himself this extremely harsh condition, he insisted on fulfilling it strictly, so he limited his time in any one city to only one night. Just as he had previously traveled humbly, so he did now, except that he added more wandering and the pains of exile.

In this way he wandered from place to place, his staff in his hand, his satchel on his shoulder, a poor wanderer like the rest of the poor, who are found in most cities where Jews live, hoping for a place at another's table. No one knew who he was and what he was doing, until he revealed himself and became the rabbinic leader of the Jewish people.

Time flew by, and after much travel, he came to a certain town late at night. He had been traveling without pause, and a cold rain poured down and penetrated his bones. The night was long and dark, one of the rainy days at the end of the month of Marḥeshvan. The town, which bore the name Pshevorsk, was small, and he had neither friend nor acquaintance there. He arrived at midnight, and the city was drenched with rain. There was mud and thick darkness, and not even a tiny sliver of light to see by. He had never been there before, he did not know any of the streets or alleys, and it was easy for a stranger to fall at every step.

So what did he do? Having no choice, he felt his way in the dark. His staff enabled him to recognize any obstacle on the path, and he peered through the blackness, looking for a house with light shining through its windows, so that he could enter and ask permission of the owner to stay overnight. He would stay in the city only one day. He would rest only for the one night, and as soon as the sun rose he would get up, wait for an hour, recite the morning prayers, and then continue on his journey, even if the rain did not stop.

But he searched in vain. Everywhere he looked there was nothing but the darkest night. The heavens above were filled with clouds, the earth below packed with black, wet mud, and the houses were locked. Not a ray of light shone through the shuttered windows. He wandered around for a long time while the rain poured down, soaking him through and through, and still he did not see a lit house. He began to be depressed but immediately felt within his depression a kind of grudge against the Jewish people, as if he were accusing them, as if among them there was not even one welcoming home for a troubled, persecuted man.

While he was thinking these thoughts, he said to himself: "It is impossible that in a city filled with Jews not one of them is awake at night studying, or another awakened for *tikkun ḥatzot,*[1] or a third getting up to recite a chapter of Psalms. And if they are not at home, then they surely are in the beit midrash. The house is cold and the beit midrash is warm, since the oven is lit. The *ner tamid* (light that is never allowed to go out) is glowing, the door is open, and whoever wants to come in can enter." As he thought of this he decided to go and search for the beit midrash, to go to sleep there for the night.

Worn out and exhausted, he continued to walk in the dark, plodding along in the muddy streets, not knowing where his feet were taking him, and every minute seemed like an hour. As he was walking he suddenly noticed a glimmer of light in the distance, and his heart rejoiced. He walked toward the light, not diverting his eyes from it, until he came to a small window in a stand-alone house, apart from the other houses in the city.

At first he thought that he had found the beit midrash, but when he tried to enter and found the door locked, he realized that he was mistaken. He approached the small window from which light was shining, and tapped on the windowpane. Immediately he heard the soft voice of a man inside asking, "Who's there?" He replied: "A Jew visiting the city, and he has no relatives here, and he is looking for a shelter from the rain and cold."

He had not yet finished speaking when he heard the screech of a bolt sliding back, and the door opened wide. He entered the house, and the man welcomed him with a broad smile, greeted him with "shalom," and he replied in kind. Then he asked the man: "Perhaps I can stay here tonight?" and the man answered: "Why not? The mitzva of *hakhnasat orḥim,* for which our father Avraham, peace and blessing be upon him, was praised has come to me unsought, and shall I not fulfill it? But before your honor goes to sleep, he should have something to eat and something hot to drink. Surely you just came from the road, and my heart tells me that you have not had dinner."

When the guest heard the kind words of the owner of the house and saw his smiling face, he said: "It is true. All day no food has touched my mouth, because during my travels I found no Jewish inn where I could taste some good food. I fasted all day against my will. Blessed be

1. Collection of psalms, confession, and other readings recited at midnight.

the good and Blessed Lord who took pity on me and brought me to the home of a Jew who wanted to fulfill the mitzva of *hakhnasat orḥim* to the full, with food, drink, and rest."

Reb Elimelekh looked around the room and saw in the middle a large table. On the table was a burning lantern, and next to that was a scribe's inkwell filled with black ink, and around it feathers made into quill pens, some of which were not finished. Near the wall, in which there was an opening to another room, was an open cabinet containing skins in various stages of being made into parchment; some were rolled like a *sefer Torah,* while others were folded and tied with light string. Near the other wall was a bed, and the pillow and blanket on it were crumpled and not made up. It looked as if someone had lain on them, gotten up, and left them as they were.

In any case, the host set the table and invited his guest to a meal. His guest did what he asked: he put down his satchel, performed *netilat yadayim* (ritual washing of hands), sat down, ate a full meal, and recited Grace after Meals. After the blessing the host said to him: "Here is the bed. A short while before you came, I got out of bed; now his honor can undress, get into bed, and rest from his hard journey." The guest did not give it much thought; he took off his outer clothing and his shoes, performed *netilat yadayim,* recited the bedtime *Keriat Shema,* got into bed, and in a very short time fell asleep.

A while later the host went into the other room, took out a book from the bookshelf, came back and sat down at the desk, and opened the book and began to peruse it. Initially the words did not make sense to him. He was reading like a man reads a book out of obligation, since all his life he was not accustomed to reading philosophical literature at this hour. But little by little he grasped the meaning of the holy words of the author, and his mind became distant from the habitual and was captured by the ideas which plumbed the depths of the tiny letters. In this way he sat, immersed in the book, and his mind was intoxicated with it. He enjoyed the words of the author as if they had been given at Mt. Sinai.

Then he heard the snoring of his guest and woke up as if from a dream. He got up, closed the book, and began to recite from memory some psalms. His voice was pleasant, and every utterance of his mouth was as sweet as a song. It was as if the Shekhina were speaking through his mouth. The words emerged with a special sweetness, vital and gleaming as on the day they were given. The words burned like fire, and he recited them from the depths of his soul. A pure, clear sound flowed into space, and some of the psalms were raised on the waves of the melody in holiness and in purity, filling the room with light and warmth.

As he awakened from his sleep, Reb Elimelekh was greatly moved to hear the voice of his host. He saw that the room was filled with light. He hastily washed his hands, dressed, got out of bed, went to the desk, and stood listening, totally in awe. The whole house was quiet; not a sound was heard except for the owner's pleasant recital.

The guest stood with open mouth, looking and listening. He was accustomed to the recitation of Psalms; his lips were accustomed to every chapter and its melody. He had heard the psalms of King David from the mouths of tzaddikim and Hasidim, but he had never experienced reading like this. Sweetness floated from the man's lips; his voice was pleasant and his melody disarming.

The master of the house threw himself into the songs of the living God, and he neither saw nor knew anything around him. His heart was stolen by the songs, which soothed his soul. And when his guest got out of bed he was unaware that he was standing near him, listening in silence to every word coming out of his mouth.

Suddenly a windstorm began to blow outside. The window shutters that were not battened down swung on their hinges loudly, and the owner stopped his singing and noticed his guest standing near the table, lost in his thoughts. "What are you doing here, my dear friend?" the host asked. "Isn't it cold in the room, and you are weary from your journey. Forgive me for awakening you from your sleep. Go back to bed, lie down and rest, and your sleep will be restful for you." But Reb Elimelekh stood still like a stone, and neither answered nor moved from his place.

When his host saw this, he grasped him by the hand and brought him back to the bed. He made him lie down and covered him well, then returned to his desk and again opened the book and perused it. The guest fell asleep again in the warm bed, since he was extremely tired, and the host began again to recite Psalms, as was his custom. This time he lowered his voice and recited the verses in a whisper, in order not to disturb his guest's sleep.

But during his recitation he became excited, and the more energized he became the more his heart followed suit, and he forgot about the man who was in his house. His soul sang out to the living God, and his voice got louder and louder, becoming thunderous, and Reb Elimelekh was awakened again. Soon he was standing beside the table as before, but this time his host saw him right away and motioned to him, without saying a word, that he should return to his bed.

Reb Elimelekh returned to his bed, but he could not fall asleep. He lay in bed resting, his eyes open, and his mind awake. His host waited a while, and then returned to his recitation of Psalms. His words were whispered and gentle. The words entered the heart of his guest, who was lying with his eyes open, half asleep, daydreaming, his soul melting with joy. At that moment it seemed as if the sound of a harp was heard in the room, and the melody of the harp was reciting psalms that were hovering and dancing in the air. He opened his eyes and saw a young man in the room. His face was the face of a shepherd, and he was a redheaded lad with beautiful eyes and beautiful to look at. He was standing next to the host, playing the harp, with white fire burning above their heads, and on the white fire chapters of the Psalms, with the musical notes, were written in red fire.

At this a great fear descended upon Reb Elimelekh, and from panic he became confused and jumped out of bed in alarm. Immediately the image of the shepherd boy disappeared, and with it also the fire above. When the host looked around and saw his guest jumping out of bed he could not hold back, but became angry at being disturbed from his work for the third time, and he ordered his guest back to bed.

Reb Elimelekh stood frightened and confused, trying to speak but unable to open his mouth. After a few minutes he regained his strength and said: "It is true that a guest must do what his host tells him, but please tell me, dear sir, is it possible for a guest to sleep in peace while he sees King David standing next to his host and singing Psalms?"

Stunned, the host exclaimed: "Who are you? You must be Elimelekh!" The guest then said: "And who are you? You must be Moshe!" The two of them fell on each other's necks out of joy, and told each other all about themselves, then sat at the table and spoke of important matters all night long.

From then on the two men were close friends. Even though Reb Elimelekh was the greater of the two and was not the same age as Reb Moshe, they joined in a deep love and friendship.

And when Reb Elimelekh returned to his home, and his light began to shine, Reb Moshe became a disciple-colleague of Reb Elimelekh, and clung to his teacher for the rest of his life.

Humans and Their Creator

GOD BROUGHT ME GOOD AND NOT EVIL

"And you shall love the Lord your God with all your heart and with all your soul and with all your might."[1]

"With all your heart" – Rashi explains: That your heart not be divided about the Almighty. "With all your might" – Rashi explains: With every measure that God metes out to you, whether for good or bad. This is the explanation of the Gemara's statement "One must bless for the evil just as one blesses for the good."[2]

Reb Zusha was moved to explain the passage on good and evil, and he did so in his unique way: "True, evil exists. Like everything else, even suffering comes from God. Why does it exist? I will tell you: Humans are too weak to accept or to digest divine grace, which is total. For this reason, and this reason alone, God camouflages it with a veil of pain."

In his extreme innocence he was not accustomed to consider anything in Creation as not testifying to God's mercy. Misery he dismissed as a figment of the imagination. Wounds were inflicted only in order to make healing possible.

1. Deut. 6:5.
2. Berakhot 9b.

ACCORDING TO ONE'S ABILITY TO SUFFER

Once, when the rabbi of Apta was crying bitterly, Reb Zusha approached him and asked: "Distinguished rabbi of Apta, why are you crying?"

"Reb Zusha, Reb Zusha, I envision great troubles on the horizon coming to our brothers the people of Israel prior to the coming of the Messiah, and that is why I am crying."

Reb Zusha replied: "Distinguished rabbi of Apta, is it a good thing to cry much? One who cries much increases sadness. Is it not written in the holy Zohar, 'Until one is able to tolerate....' The Blessed Holy One sends punishments only in a measure that one can bear."

Hearing this, the rabbi of Apta again broke down crying even more bitterly than before, and shouted: "So does Reb Zusha know how much a Jew can bear, if the Holy Blessed One metes out a measure of pain according to one's ability to suffer?"

OUR FATHER OUR KING

It happened that Reb Elimelekh of Lizhensk encountered a caravan of travelers on their way to Warsaw. He said to them: "May I ask a favor? Please ask about the welfare of my father."

"Who is he?" they asked.

"My Father is also your Father," answered Reb Elimelekh. "He is our Father in heaven."

TAKING GOD TO COURT

Word was brought to Reb Elimelekh's court of an imperial decree that would bring great hardship to the Jews of Galicia. On hearing this, one of Reb Elimelekh's students jumped up and said, "Rabbi, I summon the Creator to a *din Torah*!" The man then clapped his hands over his mouth in fright at his own words, but Reb Elimelekh calmly agreed.

He summoned Rabbi Yisrael of Kozhnitz and Rabbi Yaakov Yitzḥak, the Seer of Lublin, to act with him as judges, and the two arrived the next day. After they had taken some refreshment, they seated themselves and invited the student to present his case.

The student was shaking. "I don't have the strength!" he said.

"I will give you the strength!" replied Reb Elimelekh.

The student then managed to state his case: "This decree treats us as servants of the imperial government. But did not the Blessed Holy One decree, 'The people of Israel are My servants'?[3] If we are God's servants, then He must grant us the freedom to serve Him even in exile."

Reb Elimelekh then said: "The Holy One, blessed be He, has addressed this in the rebukes of Moshe and the prophets, and we may take those words as His answer. It is the law that after presenting their case both parties must leave the room so as not to influence the decision of the judges. It is true, God, that we cannot send You out since the whole world is filled with Your glory, and were You to withdraw Your presence we could not survive for even a moment. However, we will not allow even Your presence to influence our decision."

The student left the room. The three judges deliberated silently, with closed eyes, for about an hour. Then they called the student back and gave their judgment: the truth was on his side.

A few days later they learned that the imperial decree had been rescinded at that very hour.

A BLESSING TO THE BLESSED ONE

Reb Zusha was very precise in his teaching. He stated: "'Blessed is the Blessed God.' With every blessing which we recite – even *hamotzi* on bread, or *shehakol* on water, or *borei peri hagafen* on wine – one must direct one's thoughts not to the bread, the water, or the wine, but rather to the Blessed God, since He is the Source of all blessing. Heaven forbid that we should bless on our own pleasure."

It happened once that Reb Zusha fasted for three days because he had blessed *hamotzi* on his own pleasure.

INTEGRITY

One should be upright on all levels.
Since it is impossible to be constantly on the same level,
One runs to and fro.
At times we fall from a high level.

3. Lev. 25:55.

So one who is not upright on the lower levels, how can he climb back up?
It is compared to a ladder whose lower rungs are broken –
It is impossible to climb on it at all.

– Reb Elimelekh of Lizhensk

THE POWER OF FAITH

"Because he trusted in the Lord, He reckoned it to him as *tzedaka*"[4] (Genesis 15:6).
To all appearances, what was so great about his believing in God?
However, "He reckoned it to him as *tzedaka*" refers to Avraham.
Namely, that Avraham would contemplate himself often,
And always felt he had a negative balance.
So when the Blessed Holy One said to him: "So shall be your offspring,"[5] he believed in God,
But he was amazed at himself: How did he merit this? And he thought that this was only God's *tzedaka*.

– Reb Elimelekh of Lizhensk

ONE SHOULD BLESS FOR EVIL JUST AS ONE BLESSES FOR THE GOOD

"And the life of Sarah ... the years of the life of Sarah" (Genesis 23:1).
"The years of the life of Sarah" – they [the years] were all equally good (Rashi).
How is it possible to say that all the years of Sarah's life were equally good?
Is it not the case that she had some years that were not good?
Many years were filled with sorrow, anguish, distress, and all manner of grief.
Exile after exile in days of famine in the land,
The incidents with Pharaoh and Avimelekh,
She was barren until the age of ninety,
And in the end the binding of Yitzḥak, her only son.
Is it really possible to comment in this way: "The years of the life of Sarah – they were all equally good"?

4. The word *tzedaka* means both "righteousness" and "charity."
5. Gen. 15:5.

So this is the plain meaning which we should understand:
Sarah, the most righteous of women, would accept distress with love and alacrity
With a full and upright heart,
And with it all she would say: "This too is for the best."
This righteous woman did not, Heaven forbid, think ill of the Blessed Holy One,
And did not get angry over her misfortune.
Rather, after each wave of trouble,
Each storm and tempest that overwhelmed her, she acquiesced,
And blessed God over the bad times just as she did over the good times.
So that's how we see that the years of Sarah's life were all equally good.

– Reb Zusha of Anipoli

EVERYTHING IS FOR THE BEST

"And God blessed Avraham in all things" (Genesis 24:1).
"And God blessed Avraham in all things" – namely, with the quality of goodness.
This is the meaning of the blessing, "Who has provided me with all my needs."
Everything that the Blessed Holy One does for me is for my needs; everything is for good,
And with this wondrous feeling, our father Avraham was blessed.

– Reb Zusha of Anipoli

PERSEVERANCE

"And God said to Moshe: Tell Aharon your brother that he is not to come at all times to the holy place" (Leviticus 16:2).
"That he is not to come at all times" – he is not to come to holy places according to times.
Namely, there are times when one is strong in holiness, and there are times when one is weak in holiness.
Rather one must be in holiness at all times
Without depending on the time.

– Reb Zusha of Anipoli

A CONDITION THAT IS POSSIBLE TO FULFILL

"I am the Lord your God who brought you out of the land of Egypt" (Leviticus 19:36).
"Who brought you out" – for this purpose (Rashi).
Master of the Universe!
It is surely true that You brought us out of the land of Egypt on condition that we fulfill Your commands;
And we, to our sorrow, have not fulfilled this condition.
But the law is that one of the seven things that a condition depends on, is that it is possible to fulfill it through an agent. "A condition that is possible to fulfill through an agent is a condition. But if it is not possible to fulfill it through an agent, it is not a proper condition."[6]
Regarding the Exodus from Egypt, is it not written: "I, and not a messenger, I and not an agent"?
And if it is not possible to fulfill it through an agent, the condition is not a condition!

– Reb Zusha of Anipoli

WHAT KIND OF GOD?

What kind of God is He?
If it were I, I would teach Him how to be.
But would it help?

– Reb Zusha of Anipoli

PERFECTION

Perfection? One can find it only in the Blessed Holy One.
He is perfect and His deeds are perfect.
With humans we always find faults,
Because a flawless human has yet to be created.

– Reb Elimelekh of Lizhensk

6. Ketubot 74a.

Humans and Their Limbs

OVERHEARD

Before Reb Zusha became well known, he would wander from place to place. The story is told that once when he was in a certain city and was sitting near the stove in the beit midrash, deep in thought, a woman came in and asked if anyone had seen her husband. Her husband had deserted her, left her as an *aguna,* and she was wandering around the area searching for him. Everywhere she went she would ask about him and describe his features.

When Reb Zusha heard the woman's question, he said to her: "Go to the guesthouse. There you will find your husband." And so it was. Everyone was amazed at this miracle, since Reb Zusha had never set foot in the guesthouse but had slept in the beit midrash.

Reb Zusha explained that there was no miracle involved. Rather, he had been to the *mikve* that morning and had heard two men talking together, and one of them told his friend that a new guest arrived at the guesthouse. "I was surprised," said Reb Zusha, "for why would this report come to me? Why would my ears hear things for which I have no need or use? As I was thinking about it, this woman came and inquired about her husband, so immediately I understood that surely this very guest I heard about today in the *mikve* was the one being sought. This is the meaning of the verse 'You shall not carry empty rumors.'[1] Here 'empty' means in vain, like an oath taken in vain. Whoever is careful not to listen to empty words, merits this – that he is not asked to hear anything but what has purpose and need."

HIS EVERY NEED

It happened once that the servant of Reb Zusha was asked, "How does your master recite the blessing 'Who provides all my needs' when he has nothing except suffering and pain?"

Reb Zusha answered him, "What does my sinful body need? It needs some suffering to purify it. This is truly 'all my needs.' It follows therefore that I should offer a blessing for this joy."

THE ANTS GET DIRTY

Reb Elimelekh would frequently punish his body, rolling in the snow and lying among ants. He became so accustomed to their bites that he felt no pain. He would say, "See, Elimelekh, how hateful is your body, such that even the ants get dirty from your flesh."

SPIRITUAL CLEANSING

No soul is black; there is only a soul that has become dirty, full of soot.
There is no body that is pure; there is only a body that is purified.

– Reb Elimelekh of Lizhensk

HOLY WORDS

Words that come from the heart, enter the heart.
This means that to the very heart from which came the words,
The words return and enter the heart and add holiness to it.

– Reb Elimelekh of Lizhensk

1. Ex. 23:1.

Humility and Pride

NO PRIDE

I will find an excuse for all the questions that the heavenly court will ask me.
They will ask me:"Did you study Torah?"
I will say: "I was an ignoramus."
They will ask me: "Did you give *tzedaka* to the poor?"
I will say: "I was poor and had nothing to give."
They will ask me: "Were you occupied with mitzvot?"
I will say: "I was busy with earning a living."
For every question I will find an answer.
But if they will ask me: "Therefore what were you proud of?"
For that I will not have an answer.

– Reb Zusha of Anipoli

A GENIUS IN CHARACTER

Reb Zusha's body was usually hurting, but his spirits were high; he was without worries and delirious with joy. Man was created to be happy, even when his tortured flesh is crying with pain.

His ability to be happy was second only to his humility. It happened once that people heard him groan: "I am not suited to direct my prayers to You; I am not suited even to direct my tears to You. Instead, listen; I will whistle. That's all."

In his eyes he was the lowest of sinners. He was convinced that if he was destined to live a very long life, it would be for the purpose of suffering and atoning for as long as possible.

It is told that every day he documented all his deeds and thoughts in a small notebook. In the evening he would read what he wrote and cry until his tears erased every remnant of what was written.

Before his death Reb Zusha said: "When I stand before the heavenly court, if they ask me why I was not like our father Avraham or like Moshe Rabbenu, I will know what to answer: It is not in my ability to be like them or on their level. But what will I answer before the heavenly court if they ask me, 'Why were you not like Zusha?'"

I IMAGINE

Reb Zusha taught: "Whenever I stood in the synagogue, in the midst of a congregation, I longed to pray with *devekut* (devotion) and with the enthusiasm of a holy flame, but I was afraid that I would reach the level, Heaven forbid, of arrogance and boasting in front of others. Therefore I imagined that the entire holy congregation that filled the sanctuary were nothing but logs from trees of the forest, which would give me no reason to boast to them."

THE EARTH IS BETTER THAN ME

Earth, O earth, you are better than me. And nevertheless I tread on you and trample on you,
But do not be angry, because I will not tread on you forever,
A time will come when I will lie under you and I will surrender to you.
– Reb Zusha of Anipoli

PRAISE THE HUMBLE WITH SALVATION

It happened once that Reb Zusha fell ill. Word spread quickly to the tzaddikim of the generation, and they prayed for the recovery of this holy tzaddik. Rabbi Aryeh Leib, "the Saba (grandfather) of Shpoli," came to visit Reb Zusha at his home in Anipoli.

Reb Zusha said to his guest: "I know that you will surely pray for me and request that God have mercy on Zusha. Therefore I ask that you not attempt to arouse mercy on me because of merits. The heart knows the bitterness of its soul, and when you begin to mention merits about Zusha, it is likely that the accuser will arise, and mention the opposite of his merits, and the loss wipes out the profit.

"Rather, say to Him: 'In such and such a city near us live seven hundred non-Jews, all of whom are healthy and strong, and they lack nothing. Zusha has the same merits as they have, so it is also fitting for him to be healthy and strong.' You may use this argument, but not more than that."

The Saba of Shpoli did what Reb Zusha demanded, and so Reb Zusha arose from his sickbed and returned to good health.

THE MAGGID'S DECISION

Reb Elimelekh and Reb Zusha argued once about the order of a person's service of God: Since a person must contemplate on the one hand the exalted greatness of Hashem, and on the other hand his own lowliness, with which one should one begin?

Reb Zusha said that a person should be, first of all, so humble that out of his humility he will later come to understand the greatness of the Blessed Creator. Reb Elimelekh said the opposite, that one should view, first of all, the greatness of the Creator, and from this he will come to the recognition of his own humility.

They brought the question to the Maggid of Mezritch, to decide between them which one was correct. The Maggid replied: "Both of you are correct – 'both these and these are the words of the living God.'[1] But the one who contemplates first his own lowliness – that is the higher level; the inner kindness rests on the one who begins with himself and not with his Creator."

HE WILL NOT GET ANGRY OR COMPLAIN

Reb Elimelekh's book *Noam Elimelekh* is one of the foundational volumes of the hasidic movement. The rabbinic masters of Hasidism who lived several generations ago showered this book with praise; people would say that even the ministering angels enjoyed it and derived great pleasure from it. No wonder that *Noam Elimelekh*

1. Eiruvin 13b.

was the target of attacks by the *mitnagdim* (opponents of Hasidism). They relegated it to a *geniza* (storage room for old, worn books containing God's name).

It happened once that Rabbi Shneur Zalman of Liadi, father of Chabad Hasidism, met one of the rabbis of the *mitnagdim,* who asked him: "Who is this Elimelekh who wrote the book *Noam Elimelekh*? This book is placed under my bench."

Rabbi Shneur Zalman replied: "I met with Reb Elimelekh many times at the home of our great teacher, the Maggid of Mezritch. If your honor would really like to know the nature of Reb Elimelekh, I am prepared to tell him briefly: Even if he placed the honorable Reb Elimelekh himself under the bench, he would not feel any insult, and he would not get angry or complain."

Such was the character of Reb Elimelekh of Lizhensk, who was the leader of the great rabbis of Hasidism in Galicia.

IMPUDENCE

When the tzaddik Rabbi Aharon Leib of Premishlan came to Reb Elimelekh for the first time and entered his room to receive a greeting of "shalom," Reb Elimelekh shouted at him: "Get out of here, sinner that you are! Get out of here! I see written on your forehead a list of your transgressions, including idolatry, incest, and murder." Rabbi Aharon Leib fled from the room.

That was the day before Shabbat. Once Shabbat had arrived, Rabbi Aharon Leib entered the beit midrash of Reb Elimelekh during the setting of the table and saw him at the head of the table in the midst of a crowded congregation. Immediately Reb Elimelekh noticed Rabbi Aharon Leib and ordered the *shamash* to place him next to him at the head of the table.

After the Shabbat meal the two of them went into a special room. Reb Elimelekh said to him: "This is your defect: at a time when greatness is needed there is weakness, and at a time when weakness is needed there is greatness."

Rabbi Aharon Leib asked Reb Elimelekh, weeping: "What is this that you are saying, Rabbi, that I transgressed all the major sins? When was I such an evil person?"

Reb Elimelekh replied: "On the day that you became a bar mitzva you went in the morning to bathe in the *mikve* before putting on tefillin. On the way a certain woman saw you, took a look at you, and said with excitement: 'May it be Your will, Master of the Universe, that I merit to bear pure children like him.' You heard what she said and you were very proud.

"Our sages taught: 'Whoever is arrogant, it is as if he worships idols.'[2] They also taught: 'Whoever is arrogant it is as if he commits incest.' It is also the way of an arrogant person to embarrass his friend in public, and this is equivalent to committing murder.[3] And every one of these sins left their mark on your forehead."

HE BECAME ARROGANT

"Do not ascend My altar by steps, that your nakedness may not be exposed upon it" (Exodus 20:23).

Regarding a person who becomes arrogant and is haughty about the good qualities within him, there comes a point when his faults are revealed as well. At the point where you find the arrogance of a person, there you can discern all of his faults. This is what is meant in Scripture: "Do not ascend My altar by steps, that your nakedness may not be exposed."

– Reb Elimelekh of Lizhensk

2. Sota 4b.
3. Bava Metzia 58b.

Jewish Festivals

ALL THE HOLINESSES TOGETHER

Rabbi Yitzḥak Luria, the Arizal, taught:
On Rosh Ḥodesh one has an extra vital force .
On Yom Tov, an extra spirit.
On Shabbat, an extra soul.
When does one have all of these together?
Thus teaches the Mishnah:
"Yom Tov of Rosh HaShana that falls on Shabbat,"
Only then all the holy forces join together,
Rosh Ḥodesh, Yom Tov, and Shabbat.

– Reb Elimelekh of Lizhensk

TASTING THE TASTE OF SHABBAT

Once Reb Elimelekh said to Reb Zusha: "Zusha, my brother, when will we be able to taste the flavor of Shabbat and be gifted with an extra soul from its sanctity? Maybe the spirit only rests on us on a Shabbat when we are attired in Shabbat clothes and set a beautiful, elegant table, with all kinds of foods and delicacies."

Reb Zusha said to him, "Today is Wednesday; let us dress in our Shabbat clothing and set the table like we do for Shabbat, and we will have proof."

So they did, and immediately they tasted the flavor of Shabbat, and the holy spirit of Shabbat descended upon them.

The two of them began to cry, and said: "When will we merit to taste the spirit of the holy Shabbat?"

They went to visit their rebbe, Rabbi Dov Ber, the Maggid of Mezritch. He said to them: "Though you may be insignificant in your own eyes, you are really great scholars. We are taught: A scholar is as holy as Shabbat. Whoever observes Shabbat, the Sabbath of Sabbaths, can maintain the holiness of the Shabbat all six days of creation. Fortunate are you that you merit to transform your weekdays into Shabbat."

HE FEARED HE MIGHT DIE

It was said about Reb Elimelekh that during the chanting of the *Kedusha* of the *Amida* on Shabbat, he would take his watch in his hand and look at it; because of the great pleasantness in reciting the *Kedusha,* he was afraid he might die of ecstasy. He had to look at some material object in order to maintain his soul in his body.

A HEAVENLY VOICE

As the time for *Kabbalat Shabbat* would approach, Reb Elimelekh would close his ears so that he would not hear all the tumult in the house and in the market, because the heavenly voice of Shabbat was arousing great fear in him.

LET YOUR MIND BE AT REST SINCE YOU SET MINE AT REST

The Hasidim of Anipoli would tell the following story:

In the Upper World their rabbi, Reb Zusha, met with Rabbi Avraham Azoulai, author of *Hesed L'Avraham.*

Rabbi Avraham said to Reb Zusha: "Zusha, my good friend, I wrote ten holy books, and they are all studied in the Upper World, and nevertheless no one ever mentions my name here. And yet when they mention the name of your honor, there is much commotion in heaven. You did not write any books; what did you do in the lower world?"

Reb Zusha replied: "I wrote no books, but every Shabbat evening I went to the kitchen and said 'Shabbat Shalom' to the women who helped prepare the Shabbat food for the Hasidim who came to Anipoli. Immediately the women in the kitchen hugged one another and asked forgiveness and pardon from each other, as one does on the eve of Yom Kippur . All this came from the great love and holiness of Shabbat with which I influenced them."

Rabbi Avraham thought deeply and said: "Then all is well."

BLESSED IS ONE WHO KEEPS A SECRET

In the days when Reb Elimelekh and Reb Zusha were wandering in exile, their father would appear to them from heaven every Erev Shabbat (Friday afternoon) and direct them where to stay during the holy Shabbat.

Once they came to a certain city, and their father appeared to them on Erev Shabbat and told them that Elimelekh should stay with the local rabbi and Zusha should stay with the local shoemaker. Reb Elimelekh went to the rabbi and asked to be housed for Shabbat, and Reb Zusha tried to find a shoemaker in the city. He searched and searched until he found his home in a hidden alley on the outskirts of the city.

The shoemaker was not home, so Reb Zusha asked the shoemaker's wife where her husband was. She told him that during the week he traveled through the surrounding villages to fix the shoes of the farmers, and he had not returned yet. Reb Zusha told her that he wanted to share their meal on Shabbat.

The shoemaker's wife replied: "We would be happy to host his honor in our home, but we are very poor. Here it is Friday afternoon and we still do not have our Shabbat needs – no *ḥallot,* no meat, no wine for Kiddush, no candles to light. The Blessed One will surely bring us our Shabbat needs, but I do not know if we can bring a guest to share in our meager meal."

Reb Zusha was certain that his father did not order him to stay in the shoemaker's home in vain. He said to her: "I do not need an elaborate meal. It will be enough for me to eat just a *kezayit* (an amount of food that is the size of an olive) to fulfill my obligation to partake of a meal on the holy Shabbat."

The wife answered him: "Since you persist in asking to be our guest for Shabbat, we shall accommodate you, if my husband agrees when he returns from the village."

The shoemaker returned from the village and greeted the guest. When he heard his request, at first he refused, but afterward he acceded on condition that Reb Zusha go with him to pray with the workmen, who begin their prayers at sunrise and finish quickly so they can rest after the meal from their tiring weekday labor. Reb Zusha agreed happily to go with the shoemaker to his minyan and to watch his conduct during the prayers. Reb Zusha watched carefully and did not find anything special in the shoemaker's service. He was a simple, coarse man in tarred boots, and his speech and prayers were as rushed as his meals; he was a vain and light fellow in all his ways.

Reb Zusha was disheartened that he did merit to see or hear anything special in the shoemaker's prayers. Did his father send him to sanctify the Shabbat at his house in vain?

The Shabbat evening meal and the *zemirot* (Shabbat songs) passed quickly. Even the morning prayers were totally uninspiring, and in the afternoon there was not an inkling of the holiness of Shabbat. After the afternoon meal Reb Zusha returned to his inn with no intention of returning to the house of the shoemaker. However, when it came time for *Seuda Shlishit* (the third Shabbat meal), he felt a strong yearning to see the shoemaker once again. He went to his house but did not find either him or his wife. He was surprised that the shoemaker was not holding a *Seuda Shlishit*. Perhaps he had gone to the minyan of the workers for *Seuda Shlishit?*

He went there and did not find him. As he stood outside, he heard in the distance a faint echo of a *niggun*. He strained his ears to hear where the *niggun* was coming from, and understood that it was coming from above. He jumped up onto the roof and saw that between the roof and the ceiling there was a large attic with a small skylight. He opened the narrow skylight and squeezed himself into the attic, where he saw some dignified-looking Jews, whose faces shone like angels, sitting in a circle, with the shoemaker in the center, reciting novel interpretations of the Torah.

The stately men looked in surprise at the uninvited guest, as if to say, "Who is this fellow here?" The shoemaker whispered to them: "Since he's here already, let him stay. He was my guest over Shabbat." Reb Zusha sat among the group, quite happy to have the opportunity to learn the Torah's secrets.

When Reb Zusha left the group, the shoemaker said to him, "Be very careful. Do not tell anyone what you saw and heard."

All through the night on Motza'ei Shabbat, Reb Zusha tossed and turned, disturbed by the power of his longing for that holy congregation. Elimelekh heard him and asked what he was so troubled about. Zusha did not answer him, so Elimelekh asked again, but Zusha did not utter a sound. All night long Elimelekh repeated his questions, but Zusha was silent. Even days later Elimelekh was amazed at Zusha's greatly changed behavior. Zusha rose to greater heights in matters of holiness, in enthusiasm, and in clinging to God. A new light shown on his face, his voice overflowed with yearning, his prayer and study were burning with fiery passion. All of his movements were testimony that he had had a revelation and had climbed higher in spirituality.

Elimelekh began to press Zusha to let him in on the wonderful secret that had caused the change in him. Finally, he asked him: "My brother Zusha, do you not remember our agreement before we set out in exile, that we would be totally devoted to one another? So where is your devotion to me? I can see that since that Shabbat in the home of the shoemaker you have a secret that you are not sharing with me."

Out of compassion for his brother, Zusha broke down and told him what he had seen and heard in the attic.

That same day they came to a certain village and asked for a place to sleep at an inn. The innkeeper saw that they looked like beggars, so he brought them into the tavern and assigned them a spot on the floor to sleep. That night a rainstorm broke out, and a high-ranking official came to the inn to stay overnight. The innkeeper brought him to his house by way of the tavern. When the official saw the two men lying on the floor, he took pity on them and ordered that they be given a bed in the inn.

The next day, when the official awakened, he announced angrily that during the night a gold watch had been stolen from him. Immediately suspicion fell on the two beggars, who by then had already left the inn. The official sent two people from the town to chase after them, and they caught them at the entrance to the next city. The official asked them angrily: "Why did you steal my watch, you evil pair? Is it proper to repay evil for good?" When they denied the deed, the official gave orders for them to be tied with ropes to his carriage and beaten with a whip. Afterward they were brought to a concealed house in the forest and handed over to a judge to be tried for theft.

The judge said to them: "You should know that the official was the very same shoemaker with whom you, Zusha, stayed on Shabbat, when you climbed up to the roof to be at the *Seuda Shlishit* in the attic and heard the Torah secrets. You were asked not to tell anything of what you saw and heard. Since you did not keep your word, Heaven sentenced you to death. But to save you from death, the official ordered to have you humiliated, so as to lighten your sentence and to permit you to live.

"Remember, Zusha, if you see miracles again, do not tell them to anyone. The Blessed Holy One stays angry with anyone who does not keep a secret."

THE PROBLEMS WERE SOLVED

Rabbi Simḥa of Bubraka was a famous, great scholar, but he was also acrimonious and disputatious, and an opponent of Hasidism. He would say that Hasidism has no virtue because it causes neglect of Torah study. He would even say: "The best healing for the soul is when one reconciles a conflict in the Torah – not to say, Heaven forbid, that the Torah has contradictions which are impossible to reconcile."

It happened once that Rabbi Simḥa took sick, and the doctors could not find a medicine for his illness. His mother decided to travel without his knowledge to Reb Elimelekh, to ask him to pray for Rabbi Simḥa.

Reb Elimelekh said to her: "Go home, and the Blessed One will send complete healing for the sick man through a certain doctor who will come soon to your city for a great celebration that will be arranged in the house of the nobleman who is the head of your city. Go to him and plead with him to visit your sick son. With the help of the Blessed One the doctor will accept your request, and after he examines your son he will give him a medicine which will bring a positive result. In a short while your son will have a complete healing."

Reb Elimelekh concluded: "And after your son returns to good health, tell him in my name to go to Anipoli to my brother Zusha to receive a blessing also from him."

The woman did so, and Reb Elimelekh's promise was fulfilled completely. Rabbi Simḥa then traveled to Anipoli in order to comply with the request of Reb Elimelekh.

On Friday he came to Anipoli. In the street he met a Jew dressed in rags, who said to him: "You are a guest in our city, and I say 'shalom' to you. And what is your name?"

"My name is Simḥa," said the guest.

"Not Simḥa, but Rabbi Simḥa. Surely you are a rabbi. The aura of the Torah shines on your face," said the simple Jew.

"Yes, I am the rabbi of Bubraka."

"Since the rabbi of Bubraka has come to our city, I am honored to request that he be my guest for Shabbat."

"Are you the chief rabbi of this city?" asked the guest.

The simple Jew did not answer. Instead he said, "I am not worthy even to be the servant of the chief rabbi."

Said Rabbi Simḥa, "But I came to your city to see Reb Zusha."

The simple Jew replied, "It is well known that Reb Zusha is very busy with preparations for Shabbat. Reb Zusha says that the holy Shabbat is an important guest – a very important guest. Perhaps he is not yet free now to receive other guests. If you will listen to me, he will first come to my house. It is a mitzva upon a Jew to prepare himself to honor the Shabbat, to review the Torah portion of the week, to cut one's nails, to go to the *mikve*, to recite the Song of Songs. And after he completes his preparations in honor of the Shabbat he can go then to be welcomed by Reb Zusha."

The simple Jew brought his guest to his house and set the table for him. Then he gave him a *Ḥumash* to review the Torah portion of the week.

Rabbi Simḥa sat and rocked back and forth over the *Ḥumash* and did not say a word. Seeing that his guest was deep in thought, his host sat next to him quietly and after a while said to him: "I am surprised that on the eve of the holy Shabbat the rabbi sits deep in thought instead of preparing himself to welcome the Shabbat and review the weekly Torah portion, as would all kosher Jews. Surely you are puzzled by a difficult and complex section with some unresolved question."

"Yes, yes," answered the rabbi, "I am perplexed by a difficult problem in the commentaries of *Tosafot* which jumped out at me and is disturbing my study of the *Ḥumash*."

The host said to him, "I am only a simple Jew, with little learning. But difficult problems just before Shabbat.... The holy Shabbat itself is the solution to all problems."

When the rabbi heard this he said: "Perhaps what you say is correct.... It is fitting that I immerse myself completely in the *Ḥumash*."

Rabbi Simḥa made up his mind to remove from his thoughts the problem and immerse himself heart and soul in the study of the weekly Torah portion. His host too began to review the *parasha* in a sweet, pleasant tune, and the words were full of light and joy.

After a while the host gave Rabbi Simḥa a pair of scissors to cut his nails, and again he became lost in thought.

"Oh, the problems, the problems," mumbled the rabbi to himself in sorrow and annoyance. "They keep jumping at me again and again,and before the holy Shabbat is when they attack me hardest."

His host called out, half in wonder, and half in anger: "The worst enemies of a man are the members of his own family – this was said about problems. It is written: 'Rise up, O Lord, and let your enemies be scattered!'"[1]

Rabbi Simḥa smiled and said: "Yes, yes, they trouble me all the time, and before the eve of the holy Shabbat much more so."

Afterward the simple Jew took his guest to the *mikve*, and they both immersed. And when they returned from the *mikve* the host said to his guest: "Right now Zusha says *shalom aleikhem* to his honor the rabbi of Bubraka Is he still bothered with problems?"

The rabbi of Bubraka searched his thoughts, and it seemed to him that all the troubling contradictions in his life were resolved, and now there were none.

"Blessed be the Holy One," said the rabbi of Bubraka. "Reb Zusha, the contradictions have all been resolved for me."

COUNT AND LIST

One year on the day before Rosh HaShana, Reb Elimelekh was sitting and worrying. He thought to himself: Can I present myself before the Blessed Holy One on the Day of Judgment? Have I not committed many

1. Num. 10:35.

transgressions? He then counted them in great detail, in his usual way in matters of religion.

In the end he said, "Therefore my broken heart will bear testimony for me on the Day of Judgment."

REPENTANCE: A VIRTUE THAT STRENGTHENS MEMORY

It happened once that a Hasid lingered in the courtyard of Reb Elimelekh for most of the month of Elul, to observe the conduct of the tzaddik during the month of mercy and forgiveness.

When Rosh HaShana approached the Hasid desired to return to his city and his home in order to celebrate the Days of Awe and the festival of Sukkot together with his wife and children. As is the custom of Hasidim, he went to see the tzaddik to receive a parting blessing before his return home.

The tzaddik asked him, as was his custom in holy matters, "Do you not have any request before the new year, may it bring us good tidings?"

The Hasid replied in a mood of humility and reverence: "In Lizhensk I learned that it is fitting for one to accept with love everything that the Blessed Holy One decrees, whether material or spiritual. However, since the rabbi has invited me to make a request for something for the new year, I ask that he pray for me that my mind and my memory be strengthened. They have recently declined greatly."

Reb Elimelekh blessed the Hasid with warm words. Among other things he said: "If you want the virtue of a good memory, you must increase your repentance. Thus we learn in tractate Yoma: 'Great is repentance, since it reaches the Throne of Glory,'[2] and we are already assured in the words of our ancient teachers: 'There is no forgetting before the Throne of Glory.'[3]

THEY ALL ATE AND WERE SATISFIED

On Rosh HaShana Reb Elimelekh had a custom of hosting fifteen Hasidim. The food was generally sufficient but not plentiful, since the tzaddik was not well-off.

---

2. Yoma 86a.
3. From the blessing of "*Zikhronot*" in the Musaf prayer for Rosh HaShana.

Once on the morning of the day before Rosh HaShana, forty Hasidim showed up instead of fifteen. "Will there be enough food for all these people?" Reb Elimelekh asked his wife.

"There is barely enough for fifteen!" she answered. He asked the same question again before Minḥa and received the same answer.

During the evening service Reb Elimelekh prayed to God with special fervor, reminding Him that He provides for all creatures. After the prayers he announced in a loud voice: "Everyone come to dinner!"

The forty guests ate their fill, and there was food left over.

ADVOCATE OF THE JEWISH PEOPLE

Reb Elimelekh's custom, like that of Rabbi Levi Yitzḥak of Berdichev, was to act as advocate of the Jewish people, especially during the Days of Awe, Rosh HaShana and Yom Kippur.

Once, on the day of Rosh HaShana, before the blowing of the shofar, he turned to heaven and said: "Master of the Universe, in the *piyut* (liturgical poem) called *L'El Orekh Din*, we recite: 'Who accepts the faithful in judgment, who shows mercy to our people in judgment.' And I, Elimelekh the son of Eliezer Lipa, permit myself to remind You, Master of the Universe, that Your sages – our sages – taught: 'Whoever acquires a Hebrew servant is as one who acquires a master for himself,'[4] since the master is obliged to fulfill for a Hebrew servant what is written, 'He is happy with you,'[5] with food and drink. And since You acquired us, the members of the Jewish nation, as servants, and as You Yourself have written in Your Torah, 'For they are My servants,'[6] behold, You are obligated according to the law to have pity on Your people on the Day of Judgment, to give Your servant food and drink and meet all their needs, in order to fulfill what it says in the verse: 'He is happy with You.'"

Another year on the first day of Rosh HaShana, after the reading of the Torah, Reb Elimelekh lifted his eyes heavenward and said: "Master of the Universe, in the section about Hagar and Ishmael, You

4. Kiddushin 20a.
5. Deut. 15:16.
6. Lev. 25:42.

wrote: 'For God has heeded the cry of the boy where he is,'[7] from which our sages learned, 'One does not judge a person except according to his deeds at that hour – "where he is" – without taking into consideration what he did before and what he will do in the future.'[8] We too, the Jewish people, Your favored people, we only ask You to judge us according to our deeds of today. Behold, we have gathered in the synagogues, in the batei midrash; we have prayed, we have poured out our hearts before You in various songs and poems, we are ready with awe and reverence to hear the sound of the shofar, as You commanded us in Your Torah. Today we fulfill Your will in every detail, and we ask of You that You judge us today according to our present deeds, and do not recall our early transgressions, and do not let any thought enter Your court of judgment about what transgressions, Heaven forbid, we may commit in the future. Conduct Yourself with us as You did with Ishmael, as You heard his voice 'where he is.'"

I SHALL LIFT THE RABBI'S TRANSGRESSIONS

Once on Rosh HaShana Reb Elimelekh went to perform *Tashlikh* together with the brilliant Hasid Rabbi Zev Wolf, author of *Leshon HaZahav*. Reb Elimelekh moved a short distance away from Rabbi Wolf in order to shake off the sins from the hem of his garment, as was the custom.

Rabbi Wolf followed him, saying, "I will see where the rabbi throws his transgressions, and I will pick them up and take them with me, since what is considered a sin in the eyes of the rebbe is a merit and a mitzva for the rest of the people."

LET'S FORGIVE EACH OTHER

Once on the day before Yom Kippur a certain Hasid came to Reb Elimelekh and annoyed the *shamash* by pressing him to let him see what customs the rabbi observed at the time of *shluggen kapores* (grasping a live chicken on the shoulder blades and moving it around one's head three times, symbolically transferring one's sins to the chicken).

---

7. Gen. 21:17.
8. Rosh HaShana 16b.

When Reb Elimelekh heard about this, he ordered that the Hasid be brought to him. Reb Elimelekh told him to take a cart right away and go to a particular village, not far from the city of Lizhensk, where he should ask a certain innkeeper to let him stay overnight.

The Hasid did as he was instructed, and when he arrived at the inn, he found a room filled with half-inebriated non-Jews and the innkeeper, a simple, crude Jew, and his crude Jewish wife serving them. The Hasid sat down quietly on a bench in the corner and watched them, pretending to be asleep.

In the middle of the night, after the non-Jews had left and the door and windows were shuttered, the Hasid saw the innkeeper pacing around the room, sighing. The innkeeper ordered his wife to hand him the ledger that was lying under the bed. She pulled out an old, torn notebook and handed it to him, and the innkeeper sat down at the table and began browsing through the book, page by page, and reading what was written on each page in a voice of weeping.

In this book were written all kinds of transgressions that he had committed during the past year: On such and such a day of such and such a week, he received a guest in an impolite manner, thus failing to fulfill the mitzva of *hakhnasat orḥim* according to halakha. On such and such a day of such and such a week he listened to the foul speech of drunken non-Jews; and on this date in that month he had strange thoughts during the recitation of his prayers. On and on the list went, page after page. After each transgression that he read from the book, he heaved a sigh, and after several of them he would cry bitterly.

After he had finished reading the book of transgressions, the innkeeper asked his wife to give him the second ledger, which was lying in the corner under another bed. Again she handed him an old, torn notebook, and he began to peruse it. The pages of this book were filled with descriptions of all kinds of worries and afflictions that he had suffered from during the year. There was not one day without aggravation and calamity.

When he had finished reading this book, he put his head on the table and pondered. Then he lifted his eyes and said: "Master of the Universe, I do not deny that I owe You a great debt. But You also owe me a great debt. I do not know which debt is larger, and who is entitled to the 'change.' The account is very heavy and extremely complicated. And since we are on the cusp of the day before Yom Kippur, which is the day of forgiveness and pardon, therefore, Master of the Universe, let's make an agreement: I don't owe You anything and You don't owe me anything. A notebook filled with transgressions for a note of pain and worries: this is my trade, this is my compensation.... *Leḥayyim*, Master of the Universe!"

Toward morning the Hasid returned to Lizhensk. When he came to Reb Elimelekh, the rabbi greeted him with a smile: "So what did you see there?"

The Hasid told him everything in detail, and the rabbi replied: "The very same thing that this innkeeper said to the Master of the Universe, King David argued before Him. And this is the plain meaning of the verse 'O Lord, all my longings lie open before You, my groaning is not hidden from You':[9] since 'all my longings lie open before You,' but also 'my groaning is not hidden from You,' therefore let us deduct one from the other, and we will forgive and pardon one another."

THE BROTHERS' ANXIETY

During the period of their exile, Reb Elimelekh and Reb Zusha came to a certain city the day before Yom Kippur and went to the beit midrash. Because of their torn clothing and the condition of all of their possessions, they appeared as lowly beggars, and thus not one person invited them to his home to have a meal. The two brothers were enveloped in sadness, because they could not fulfill the teaching of *Ḥazal* (the sages of the Mishna and Talmud) that whoever eats and drinks on the day before Yom Kippur is credited with having fasted two days of Yom Kippur.

An hour later a young man entered the beit midrash and asked them if they had finished the meal that precedes Yom Kippur. When he learned from them that they had not yet eaten, he said to them: "What can I do for you, fellow Jews, since I and my family have already finished our meal, and there is absolutely nothing left in our house?"

9. Ps. 38:10.

The young man went to a store and bought some cakes and schnapps. They ate and drank, and thanked the Blessed One who arranged that this fine young man would enable them to partake of the *seudat mitzva* (ritual meal) before the holy day.

The following year the two brothers happened to come again, through God's providence, to the same city on the day before Yom Kippur. And as in the previous year, not one person among those praying in the beit midrash paid any attention to the two beggars, until the same young man honored them with cake and schnapps.

Strange are the ways of the Almighty. For a third consecutive year the two brothers happened to visit the same city on the day before Yom Kippur. To their great sorrow the young man did not show up at the beit midrash. Their depression was intense. They were sad about the desecration of the holiness of the ninth of Tishrei, and also overwhelmed with worry over the fate of the young man. They longed to see him face-to-face, but he was nowhere to be found.

Zusha said to his brother: "Do you not think, my brother, that it is our duty to search for this young man, whom the Blessed One sent to us twice to enable us to perform the holy mitzva of the ninth of Tishrei?"

Elimelekh answered: "Zusha, my brother, what can Elimelekh do, since he is blind and cannot see anything? Zusha's eyes are bright; maybe you can see where the young man is."

Zusha said: "Zusha, who is lowly and disgraceful, is searching everywhere and does not see anything. But you, my brother, are not looking anywhere, and yet you see far into the distance. Even what is hidden from Zusha is known to you."

Elimelekh said: "Elimelekh does not see and does not know anything, but sometimes when Zusha my brother sees, Elimelekh also knows."

Zusha said: "Come, my brother, let us search for the young man throughout the world."

The two of them were engrossed with different thoughts and ideas. They searched for him throughout the world but did not find him. They explored more ideas. Zusha suggested: "Let us go, my brother, and search in the Upper World." They searched for him in the Upper World. They thought more deeply. They found him standing on the tower of a Christian church. They said: "Woe to the soul of this young man, for such a terrible thing to happen to him. Twice he gave food and drink to two beggars the day before the holy day."

Zusha said: "Elimelekh, my brother, you have a holy mouth. Pray for this Jewish soul, that it not, Heaven forbid, be lost."

Elimelekh said: "Elimelekh is lowly and disgraced. But you, Zusha my brother, place the words of your kind heart on the lips of Elimelekh, and the two of us together shall pray to the Blessed One for this Jewish soul, to save it from the trap of the *sitra aḥra*,[10] may Heaven protect us."

A PURE PRAYER

It happened once that Reb Zusha of Anipoli entered the beit midrash during *Kol Nidrei* and felt the great warmth and enthusiasm with which the congregation recited this pure prayer.

Reb Zusha approached the *aron hakodesh* (holy ark), lifted his eyes heavenward, and said: "Master of the Universe! If it were only for this alone it would be worthwhile for the Jews to sin. For if we had not sinned, where and when would You hear heartfelt and passionate prayers like these?"

A HOLY MAN

When he was a young man the tzaddik Rabbi Neta of Chelm would frequently visit Reb Elimelekh during the time that he served as a teacher to the two sons of a villager. The pupils were ignorant and boorish, and they did not achieve great benefit from their studies, but the tzaddik did what he was supposed to do, and studied with them every day, well into the night. When the family slept, he stayed and worshipped the Blessed Holy One in his room with deep devotion, unbeknownst to anyone.

When he sat at the table to eat with the family on Shabbatot and holidays, he would hold a scarf in his hand. He would pretend to be eating, but he actually put all the food into the scarf. After the meal he went outside, and what was fit to throw away, he threw away, and what was fit to eat, he hid in his room. And on Shabbat evenings, when the family went to sleep, he would go to his room to recite *Kabbalat Shabbat* (welcoming the Sabbath) and the evening prayers. Then with devotion and joy, he

10. Literally, the "other side," referring to the forces of evil.

would set the table with the two *ḥallot,* recite Kiddush over them, and eat a meal there in a holy way. He would do the same the next morning.

It happened once that the woman of the house awakened in the middle of the night and heard a loud noise. She was very frightened, so she got out of bed and walked toward the noise. Behind the teacher's door she heard him praying *Kabbalat Shabbat* with sweetness and enthusiasm, such that her soul almost took flight. The next day she began to scrutinize the teacher's actions and noticed striking peculiarities in his eating and other actions. The woman understood that the teacher was not a simple man but rather a holy person. She related the matter to her husband, and he too began to watch and observe the teacher's actions and understood that the teacher was a hidden tzaddik.

After discussing the matter, the couple went into the teacher's room and said to him: "You can no longer hide your holy deeds from us, since we know well your holy behavior and ways of being. We have therefore come to request that you remain with us, and act in whatever way your heart desires, and you will lack for nothing, since we shall be here to serve you and pay you generously with honor. And with regard to your teaching responsibilities, we see that our sons will not be outstanding students of Torah, and it is sufficient for us if they know the weekly Torah portion, *Ḥumash* with Rashi, and some words of *musar* (Jewish ethics). So when you have free time, you can teach them some words of Torah and *musar,* and we would like it if they can learn from you to have love and awe of God and His Torah. But you should not interrupt your holy work all the time for our sons." The tzaddik agreed, and so they did what was suggested.

Little by little the residents of the village began to find out about him, and related to him as the holy man that he was. Word of his holiness spread, and eventually the people in the next village of Vladova heard about him and several young men began to travel to him from this town to enjoy the sparks of his teachings. The owner of the house would give them food and drink and serve them, and God blessed him and the work of his hands, and he became very wealthy and influential, and he used these gifts in good ways.

Time passed, and the owner of the house where the tzaddik had stayed was dragged down little by little, until he became totally impoverished. He conferred with his wife about what to do, since they had already sold all their property and consumed all their wealth and possessions, and there was nothing left in their home. His wife recalled some memories from the early days and told her husband: "Please, my husband, listen to my advice. Surely you heard that the rebbe, Rabbi Neta, who once taught our sons, has now become a great tzaddik and is famous as a miracle worker. Go see him; surely he will remember us and all the good we bestowed upon him, and he will bring us salvation and mercy."

The husband listened to his wife's advice and went to Chelm. He imagined that when he would reach the doorstep of the home of the tzaddik, immediately Rabbi Neta would run to welcome him, remembering all the good things that he once did for him. But it did not turn out the way he thought. When he came to the home of the tzaddik, he found many people waiting for him. And when the tzaddik's door opened, and they all went to receive a welcome, he too was in the crowd of comers. The rebbe wished him "shalom" exactly as he did to everyone else. The man was discouraged, but he gave him the benefit of the doubt, thinking that it was the day before Shabbat and the rebbe was very busy, having no free time to greet him. But even on the night of Shabbat when he sat among the rest of the Hasidim at the table, the tzaddik showed him no sign of recognition, and the same thing happened in the morning and later at *Seuda Shlishit.*

After Shabbat the poor man went in to see the rebbe to receive a parting blessing. He gave him a note, as was the custom, and the rebbe blessed him with "shalom," just as he blessed all the other men.

The man could not restrain himself. He said to the tzaddik, "I have one question that I would like to ask the rabbi."

The rabbi replied: "Ask, my son, ask."

The man said: "All year long we ask God to answer our prayers because of *zekhut avot* (the merit of our forefathers). During the days of *Seliḥot,* preceding the Days of Awe, we say: 'Remember the covenant of Avraham and the binding of Yitzḥak.' Also on Rosh HaShana and during the ten days of repentance and on Yom Kippur we ask the Blessed Holy One to save us because of *zekhut avot.* At the end of the Days of Awe during *Ne'ila,* the time of sealing our fate, when we add an additional prayer that we do not recite the entire remainder of the year, we have a chance to call up some new merit, and we say right at the beginning of the *piyutim* (liturgical poems), 'Father knew you from youth.' Thus we recite *zekhut avot* all the time, so what is new now?"

The tzaddik replied, "Surely you have some explanation for this. Please tell me, my son, what is your opinion on this?"

"I think that at the final sealing of our fate we are afraid perhaps they will say in heaven: What's all this noise about *zekhut avot?* That if it weren't for the forefathers we would not know about the greatness of the Creator, who created and sustains everything in heaven and on earth? For this we add: 'Father knew you from youth,' namely, it is true that without the forefathers the Blessed Creator sustains and supports everything, but at the time of the forefathers the world lacked anyone who acknowledged His greatness, and our father Avraham is the one who showed His nature in the world, that all should recognize and know this.

"And I too say so," added the man. "The rebbe was also a holy man, but years ago who had known him, and who had heard of him? Was it not I who made known to the world his name? Then why does the rabbi not worry about me, now that I am poor and without anything?"

The tzaddik was very happy to hear the thoughts of the man, and said to him, "Go in peace, my son, and from now on the Blessed One will help you in your affairs."

Very soon the man became wealthy again and lived a long and pleasant life. The tzaddik often told his friends about the man's past and praised his words greatly. And the Hasidim said: "Not without reason did the tzaddik not show favor to the man nor welcome him graciously. He wanted to prompt him to recite the phrase 'Father knew you from youth.'"

THUS HE SAID

On Yom Kippur before the *Ne'ila* prayer, Reb Elimelekh brought charges against his Maker, saying: "Master of the Universe, through Your prophet Isaiah ben Amotz You asked us: 'Where is the bill of divorce of your mother whom I dismissed?'[11] This means that You, Lord our God, admit

11. Is. 50:1.

Yourself that You bound us in a bond of marriage, as a woman is bound to her husband when we recite in the engagement blessing 'Who sanctifies His people Israel through *ḥuppa* and *kiddushin*.' Is it not the law that the husband is obliged to give his wife several things, including food, clothing, and healing, and also to redeem her if she is captured?[12] And so the members of Your people Israel, whom You sanctified through *ḥuppa* and *kiddushin*, turn to You and require that You pay Your debt: to give us bread to eat and clothing to wear, and heal us and we shall be healed, and if we are captured now among the nations, You are required to redeem us.

"Lest You say that we sinned, we have gone astray, and committed iniquity before You, and Your obligations to us are nullified, have not our sages taught that 'a person does not commit a transgression unless the spirit of foolishness has entered into him,'[13] and is it not a law that 'one who marries a woman and later deserts her is obligated to provide for her food and healing, everything according to what one was required to give her before'?"

IN YOUR HAND IS THE MATTER

"Behold as the clay in the hand of the potter...
so are we in Your hand, O God" *(Piyut* for Yom Kippur).
From clay we make bricks, whether for a palace or for a prison....
"So are we in Your hand, O God."
From a little bit of Jewish clay You can, Master of the Universe,
Raise a beautiful building that will glorify the world.
And You can, if You want, build from it a wretched and shabby cottage...
It is the very same clay, the very same bricks....

– Reb Zusha of Anipoli

"FROM GOD THE STEPS OF A MAN ARE PREPARED"[14]

Once during Reb Zusha's years of wandering it happened that he found himself in a certain village on the day before the festival of Sukkot. He was distressed because he did not know if he would find a kosher sukka and the four species. He was walking through the village, searching for

12. *Shulhan Arukh, Even HaEzer,* chapter 69, paragraphs 1 and 2.
13. Sota 3a.
14. Ps. 37:23.

a Jew, and the people there directed him to a merchant who lived on a hill on the outskirts of the village.

Reb Zusha went to him and asked him if he had a sukka and the four species, and the merchant nodded his head. Reb Zusha went to get ready to welcome the festival, bathing in the river and changing his clothing, and when he returned and the merchant brought him into the sukka, he stood there in amazement: several candles were already burning, and the sukka was completely covered with gleaming white sheets, with all kinds of flowers and fruit that emitted an aroma of *Gan Eden*. The merchant recited Kiddush, performed the ritual hand washing, and in the middle of the meal got up, gazed heavenward, and said: "Master of the Universe, You commanded us to rejoice on the festival, as it is written: 'You shall rejoice on your festivals,' and here I am a lone Jew in the village, so how can I rejoice? I know the joy of a father who tells his son to dance and he does so, and if I, Master of the Universe, can bring You joy, this alone will fill me with great joy!"

Then the merchant danced with great enthusiasm until he was exhausted. After that he took the cup in his hand and drank a bit of wine that was left from Kiddush, and again looked heavenward and said: "Master of the Universe, You have long life, Your sustenance is not lacking, enemies do not have the power to harm You, so how can I bless You? May it be Your will that You reap satisfaction from Your children, the people of Israel."

Reb Zusha thought: It seems that not without reason did I happen to come here. It is so I will know what service of God is. I can testify that when the merchant danced, the entire host of heaven danced with him. There has not been this kind of joy ever before, since he fulfilled the mitzva of 'You shall rejoice in your festivals' without any reason other than to fulfill the mitzva of the Torah. How fortunate am I that I am with him!

IN THE FUTURE

Following his custom, on the festival of Sukkot Reb Zusha would bring several simple folk and untutored men to his home, to give them food and drink and to rejoice together with them.

Some of his friends asked him why he did this, and he replied: "In the future, when tzaddikim will sit in the sukka made of the skin of

Leviathan (a giant mythical sea creature), Zusha will also go, and he will want to join them and enter the sukka, but they will not let him. They will say: Should you, Zusha the simple one, merit to sit in the place where tzaddikim sit? Now Zusha can come and argue: he too brought simple folk and unlearned men into his sukka."

TRUE ILLUMINATION

Reb Elimelekh forbade strong drink during the closing days of Sukkot, lest an alien element contaminate the joy of holiness. For there are people who drink a lot of liquor in order to have a spiritual illumination, but this light is from *klipat noga,*[15] and one must distinguish between this false light and the light of the Torah, which brightens the eyes and makes the heart rejoice. Not all things that shine are gold. Even a decayed piece of wood shines in the darkness of night.

SAVE US

Reb Zusha of Anipoli taught on the day of Hoshana Rabba: Any other nation who would linger in a bitter exile for a thousand and eight hundred years, would they have any remnants left? They would desert their religion and forget their gods. But Israel is a holy nation; they suffer again and again, have faith again and again in the unity of the Creator, until death. We chant "Save us for the sake of Your unity." Save us so that the belief in Your unity will remain. Save us so our feet do not slip. Save us!

REVEALED MIRACLE

"But the Israelites walked through the sea on dry ground" (Exodus 14:29). People are amazed when they see things which are outside the realm of nature, revealed miracles,
And they do not understand that nature itself is one huge miracle,
That one can always see the greatness of the Creator and get excited over it.
But when one sees a revealed miracle they begin to believe

15. In kabbalistic thought, this refers to one of the "husks" that conceal the divine light. Unlike the three "husks of uncleanness," *klipat noga* is not entirely evil but is a place where good and evil are intermingled.

That in the everyday simple and natural life, every day,
There exists divine providence, and miraculous things happen,
But we are accustomed to them, and we don't pay attention to them.
This is what is meant in the Torah verse: "But the Israelites..."
When they saw a revealed miracle, like when they walked through the sea on dry land,
They came to realize that "walking through the sea on dry land,"
Even walking on solid, dry land,
Is as wonderful a miracle as if they were walking through the sea.

– Reb Elimelekh of Lizhensk

Kindness and Mercy

IN THE MERIT OF OUR ANCESTORS

Rabbi Eliezer Lipa, the father of Reb Zusha and Reb Elimelekh, was a wealthy tax collector who lived in one of the villages near Lvov. He was well known in the area as a charitable man whose door was always open. When he traveled from the village to the city and back, he would take into his carriage any poor person he met on the road and bring him wherever he wanted to go.

It was told that once while traveling to Lvov he met a poor man trudging along on the road with his satchel on his shoulder. Rabbi Eliezer Lipa suggested that he get in the wagon and travel together with him to the city. The poor man refused, saying, "I prefer to walk on foot, and on my way I go into every village, stop at Jewish homes, and collect charity."

Rabbi Eliezer Lipa asked him: "How much money do you expect to collect for yourself during your travel through the villages, before reaching Lvov?"

The poor man answered, "My estimate is that I can collect at least twenty-five gold coins, and it would be a shame for me to lose that amount if I ride with you on the wagon directly to Lvov."

Rabbi Eliezer Lipa wanted to give him twenty-five gold coins from his own pocket to save him the trouble of going from village to village, but the man still refused, saying, "I've known the Jews who live in these villages for many years, and they know me. I already have a ritual of going to them from year to year to collect their handouts. If I travel in your wagon directly to Lvov and skip these villages, the Jews who live there will think that surely some tragedy befell me, and why should I cause them sorrow for nothing?"

"If that be the case," said Rabbi Eliezer Lipa, "do me a favor. Place your satchel in my wagon. I will bring it to the city and hand it to my innkeeper, and it will be kept with him until you arrive and take it."

The poor man was hesitant until Rabbi Eliezer Lipa gave him a very generous amount of charity; then he agreed to give him the satchel so he could bring it to Lvov in his wagon.

It is said of Rabbi Eliezer Lipa that he was very proud of his Jewishness, and every morning, when he recited the blessing "Blessed ... who has not made me a non-Jew," he would dance for joy. He was the only Jew in all the villages around Lvov who would not bow down before the land-owning noblemen. He would not curry favor with them, and he would speak to them with firmness out of pride in his heritage. Because of this they would treat him with honor and respect.

Once he was riding on his horse to one of the nearby villages. Suddenly a luxurious carriage harnessed to four stallions blocked his path. In it sat a nobleman and his wife who did not know Rabbi Eliezer Lipa. The nobleman stopped him and asked, "Where are you from, Jew?"

"From such and such a village," answered Rabbi Eliezer Lipa calmly.

The nobleman saw that here was a Jew who did not remove his hat in subservience, and he became angry and yelled, "Your hat, Jew!"

"The hat is also from such and such a village," replied Rabbi Eliezer Lipa in a gentle mocking voice, and calmly struck his horse with the whip and continued on his way.

Rabbi Eliezer Lipa was involved in redeeming captives among the Jewish people, who rented and paid taxes and were taken captive by tyrant noblemen. Once it became known to him that a certain nobleman from a nearby village had put his Jewish tax collector in jail because he did not pay the rent on time. Rabbi Eliezer Lipa harnessed his horse to the wagon, took with him all the money he had, and traveled to the nobleman in order to redeem the captive. When he reached the palace he found out that the debt of the tax collector was several thousand gold coins, and Rabbi Eliezer Lipa had only half the amount of the debt. He pleaded with the nobleman and finally persuaded him to take the half and free the tax collector. When Rabbi Eliezer was about to take leave of the nobleman, the nobleman said to him: "I see that you are an honest man with a good heart, and I am confident that you do business in good faith. In a nearby village lives a member of my family, a wealthy nobleman with much property. He has a great deal of merchandise to sell – wheat, barley, and flax – but he is searching for another honest merchant upon whom he can rely. I will give him your letter, and he will sell you his merchandise."

"I thank you very much, my lord nobleman, for your kind heart," Rabbi Eliezer Lipa said to him, "but I do not have any funds with which to buy things. All the money that I have I paid you to cover the debt of the tax collector."

"If so," said the nobleman to him, "I will return your money to you. You can travel to my relative the nobleman, and buy his merchandise from him. And I trust that when you make a profit, you will return the money to me that I am giving you now."

Rabbi Eliezer Lipa took the money together with the letter and traveled to the nobleman. The nobleman read the letter and agreed to sell to Rabbi Eliezer Lipa his merchandise at a reasonable price. He sent his servant with him in order to show him the merchandise.

On the way Rabbi Eliezer Lipa heard someone crying. "Who is crying?" Rabbi Eliezer Lipa asked the servant.

"It is a Jew," said the servant. "Several days ago the nobleman imprisoned him because he didn't pay his debts, and he decided to starve him to death."

Rabbi Eliezer Lipa returned immediately to the nobleman and paid him the money the Jewish man owed with the money he had with him. When the man had been freed, Rabbi Eliezer Lipa prepared to go home.

"So what about the business deal between us?" asked the nobleman.

Rabbi Eliezer Lipa stood up straight and tall, gave him a sharp, piercing look, and said to him: "I will tell you the truth. Once I found out how cruelly you treated that Jew, I decided that I will not do any business with you, even if I could have earned great profits."

A feeling of shame mixed with respect went through the heart of the nobleman when he heard Rabbi Eliezer Lipa's words, and his face reddened. He looked in the honest and righteous face of Rabbi Eliezer Lipa, and began to apologize, saying: "You are right. I behaved badly, and I promise you that from now on I will change my ways for good. This is the sign: The money that I gave for payment of the debt of the Jew, I am giving you credit on the bill for the merchandise we exchange. We will do business in the future, and I hope that you will be satisfied with me."

Rabbi Eliezer Lipa bought the merchandise and profited from this sale, and in a short time he was able to repay the first nobleman.

FREEDOM FOR THE BIRDS

Reb Zusha of Anipoli would travel around the towns and villages to collect funds to redeem captives, that is, to pay the ransom for Jews who were punished with imprisonment due to not paying the exorbitant taxes forced on them by the hard-hearted noblemen.

Reb Zusha came to an inn in a village, but did not find anyone there. He walked through the inn, and saw in one of the rooms a cage full of birds. Watching the birds in the cage, he got the feeling that it was not comfortable for them there, and that they had no joy in this dwelling place. Reb Zusha said: "It is obvious that their souls long to go out and fly to the heavens. For is this not the will of the Blessed Holy One, who made them with wings?"

Reb Zusha then said: "Come see, Zusha, what is written about the Creator, that 'His mercy is upon all His works.'[1] And are these birds not the work of the hands of the Blessed Holy One?"

He continued: "Zusha, Zusha, a mitzva came to you inadvertently to proclaim freedom to these wretched birds. And this is an easy mitzva which you do not have to labor over. Oh, Zusha, Zusha, why are you standing and gaping? Get up and do something. Do you not pound your feet on the roads to fulfill the mitzva of redemption of captives? Zusha, you love mitzvot, and not because you are a tzaddik, but because you want the reward of a place in the World to Come. Evil Zusha, do you only labor to save souls for the sake of your share in the World to

1. Ps. 145:9.

Come? These birds are also captive. Zusha, do not be lazy. Get up and break the cage, and free these poor souls." Reb Zusha broke open the cage and fulfilled the mitzva of *shiluaḥ haken.*[2] The birds flew out, and Zusha also went outside. He walked about in the courtyard and watched the flight of the birds.

When the innkeeper returned he was astonished to see the broken, empty cage. He went out to the courtyard and noticed a stranger walking around and gazing at the sky.

The innkeeper asked him, "Who are you?"

Reb Zusha answered, "Zusha the evil am I. *Shalom aleikhem,* my brother. You must also wish me "shalom," since I am also a Jew.

The innkeeper said to him, "I do not know if you are a tzaddik or an evil person, but I suspect that you are a fool in any case. Was it not you who broke the cage and set the birds free?"

"Yes, Zusha did it."

The innkeeper shouted, "Empty-headed fool that you are, how did you dare to free my birds from the cage? They cost me a lot of money! I will break your bones!"

Reb Zusha replied gently, "Reb Jew, do you recite the obligatory prayers every day?"

The innkeeper stared at him in amazement. "Yes, I recite the prayers," he answered. What is the connection of prayers to this matter, fool that you are?"

"And in your prayers you recite about the Blessed Holy One: 'His mercy is upon all His works.'"

"Mercy, mercy!" cried the innkeeper in a fury. "But on a fool, it is said, it is forbidden to have mercy."

He slapped Reb Zusha's face and threw him out of the courtyard. And Reb Zusha went on his way to fulfill the mitzva of redeeming captives.

REWARD FOR EFFORT

Once the wife of Reb Zusha urged him to have a new dress sewn for her. He could not resist her pleas, so despite his poverty, he borrowed

2. Sending away the mother bird (see Deut. 32:6).

money and bought her fabric for a dress. His wife gave the fabric to a tailor. Since Reb Zusha considered that his wife's annoyance had subsided, his mind was at rest. But several days later he noticed again that his wife looked dejected. When he asked her why she was angry again, she related to him the following story:

"It is true that I gave the fabric to a tailor, and he sewed a proper dress for me, but when the tailor brought the dress I saw that he was downcast, and I heard his brokenhearted sighs. I asked him: 'What is the reason for your broken heart, Reb Yid?' The tailor replied: 'I see this beautiful dress, and I am reminded of my poor daughter's anxiety. A while ago my daughter became engaged, and the date of the wedding was approaching. The groom saw that I was sewing a beautiful dress, and he was certain that I was sewing it for my daughter in preparation for the wedding. When he found out that it was not so, he became very angry and no longer looked favorably at me and my daughter. My daughter noticed this, and her heart was broken. She feared lest he would cancel the wedding. And I do not have a heart of stone. When my daughter feels pain, I too have pain, and the whole world looks bleak.'

"When I heard this, immediately I told the tailor that I would give him the dress as a gift for his daughter the bride. I am not a bride waiting to stand under the *ḥuppa,* and my Zusha will not divorce me if I don't have a beautiful dress. The tailor took the dress and departed. I did a mitzva. But I am sad that I am wearing rags as always. It is a disgrace for me to be seen in public."

Reb Zusha told her: "Forget the dress. Those who do righteous deeds should not be ashamed. How fortunate you are, my wife, that you overcame your *yetzer hara* (evil inclination) in the guise of a beautiful garment. But did you give the tailor a reward for his labor?"

His wife stared at him in astonishment and said, "Is it not enough that I gave the tailor the dress? Must I also give him a reward for his labor?"

"Think for yourself, my wife. The poor tailor labored a whole week for you, just for you, to earn his wages. He depended on this dress to sustain his family for the whole week, and if you do not compensate him, you are withholding the wage of a worker. The gift is one thing and the payment is another."

Immediately Reb Zusha went and borrowed money to pay the fee to the tailor.

PERPETUAL KINDNESS

"I thank you, Lord our God and God of our ancestors,
For all the kindness which You have bestowed upon me,
And which You will bestow upon me in the future,
And upon all of my family" (Prayer before Kiddush on Friday night).
"For all the kindness which You have bestowed upon me" – the appreciation is understood,
But why the thanks for the kindness "which You will bestow upon me in the future"?
I know You, Master of the Universe, the pillar of kindness, that You will continue to show me kindness.
But I am afraid that in the future, I might not realize or be aware of Your kindness, and will not be able to appreciate it and thank You for it.
Therefore, now, when I know and witness that it is true, I already thank you for the future – in advance.

– Reb Elimelekh of Lizhensk

The Totality of the Jewish Nation

OPENING WITH A BLESSING

Every morning on waking, before he said a word to the Blessed One or to any person, Reb Zusha was accustomed to call out: "Good morning to all Jews!"

During the day he would write a list of everything he did on a sheet of paper, and in the evening, before going to bed, he would read the list and would cry so much that the writing would be effaced by the tears.

THE EXPLANATION OF THE BLESSING

The author of the book *Daat Moshe,* Rabbi Moshe Eliakim Beria of Kozhnitz, who was the leading pupil of Reb Zusha and spent much time with him, testifies in his book, in *Parashat Ekev,* that Reb Zusha was accustomed to bless every Jew with these words:"May you be as healthy and strong as a non-Jew!"

He would sometimes add, to explain the depth of the meaning which is hidden in this blessing, "Not only because the crude non-Jew is strong in body and sturdy in health, but mainly because the non-Jew achieves his good health without justification and without having deserved it at all. How much more so, therefore, are holy Jews worthy to be healthy and strong, seeing that even the empty-headed among them are as full of mitzvot as there are seeds in a pomegranate."

Qualities of Character

WHO REMEMBERS THE LOVING-KINDNESS OF OUR ANCESTORS

On his wanderings Reb Elimelekh dressed as an ignorant villager, unkempt and sporting a wispy beard. Once, when he arrived at the city of Czernowitz, he went to the local community leader and requested permission to preach in the synagogue. The leader refused. Reb Elimelekh pleaded with him, and the leader threw him out of his house.

When the son of the community leader, Avner, saw his father expel the preacher from his house, he began to plead with his father, saying: "What do you care, Father, if this poor man earns a little money for his sermon? When a Jew comes and requests permission to preach, it is clear that he knows how to preach. Father, give him permission to deliver his sermon."

The community leader listened to his son and fulfilled his request. He called the poor man back to his home and handed him a note to give to the *shamash* of the synagogue. The *shamash* notified all the local citizens that a preacher was coming who would give a sermon in the synagogue that night.

Everyone in town came to the synagogue. Reb Elimelekh ascended the pulpit, looked all around in amazement, and did not say a word. The congregation became angry. Several leading members of the congregation approached the preacher and asked him: "Why are you not preaching? And why are you looking around? Are you searching for someone?"

Reb Elimelekh said: "Yes, I am looking, my brothers. I am searching for a sign of fear of God here, and I can't find one. My fellow Jews, I am looking here and there, and see a *Gehinom* of sinners burning all over. Sinners that you all are, repent!"

Immediately the synagogue broke out in pandemonium. The angry congregants jumped on the pulpit to beat Reb Elimelekh. Reb Elimelekh jumped off the podium and ran out of the synagogue. They chased him out of town and then returned to the city.

Unlike the others, young Avner continued to run after him until he caught up to him, and said to him, weeping, "Preacher, wait a minute!"

Reb Elimelekh stopped and said to the young man, "What do you want, my son?"

The boy replied, "Here is my pouch of money. Please take it from me as payment for the sermon."

Reb Elimelekh said to him, "But this money is your father's, and you don't have the right to give it away."

The young man replied, "The money was my father's, but now it is mine. I am an only child. Every day my father gives me some coins as a gift, and I have accumulated a large sum. Now they are mine, and I request that you receive them from me as payment for the sermon."

Reb Elimelekh accepted the money, placed his hand on the young man's head, and said to him, "How can I bless you, my son?"

The boy said, "Any blessing that you give me will be good in my eyes."

Reb Elimelekh blessed him that one day they would be in-laws. The boy did not ask the preacher his name.

Avner grew up and married, and one of his daughters became engaged to a grandson of the rabbi of Apta, who was also a grandson of Reb Elimelekh. In honor of the rabbi of Apta, seventy famous rabbis came to Zarnowitz where the wedding was held. Among them were the Seer of Lublin and Rabbi Yaakov Yitzḥak of Peshischa, the Yehudi HaKadosh. Reb Elimelekh had already left this world.

When the rabbi of Apta arrived in Zarnowitz, he sent someone to call his in-law, Avner. When Avner entered the inn, the rabbi of Apta arose before him and said, "I see light in your face, Reb Avner."

After they had arranged matters of the *ḥuppa* and marriage ceremony, the rabbi of Apta asked: "Please tell me, Reb Avner, who are you and what have you achieved, that you have merited to marry into the family of the grandson of Reb Elimelekh, of blessed memory?"

Avner replied, "I don't know, dear rabbi. I am just a simple Jew, but I respect rabbis."

The rabbi of Apta replied, "Yes, you are a simple Jew, but it seems that your family welcomes guests."

Avner replied humbly, "Yes, honored rabbi, I never refuse poor people in my house."

The rabbi of Apta said, "You are surely a generous person who gives much *tzedaka,* Reb Avner."

Avner replied innocently, "I give *tzedaka,* but not much."

The rabbi of Apta replied, "You are a very generous donor, but nevertheless I do not know how you merited to have married into the family of Reb Elimelekh of Lizhensk, the outstanding tzaddik. It is not sufficient to be one who welcomes guests, gives much *tzedaka,* and is a God-fearing Jew to merit marrying your daughter to a descendant of Reb Elimelekh, who was not flesh and blood, but a pure angel. Tell me more, Reb Avner, about who you are and what your family has done in your lives. Tell me everything from the first day of your life that you can remember. What mitzva did you do when you were a young man?

Avner dug deeply into his memory bank and recalled the pouch of money he had given to a poor preacher when he was very young.

The rabbi of Apta said, "And what did that poor preacher look like?"

Avner said that he was wearing ragged clothing with a straw belt, and had a wispy beard.

The rabbi of Apta exclaimed, "Yes! That was Reb Elimelekh; yes, that was the one, may his memory be for a blessing."

Avner delved deeper into his memory. Suddenly his face lit up with great clarity, and he said with embarrassment, "I also remember the blessing he gave me, may his memory be blessed, that we will be related by family."

Said the rabbi of Apta: "That is not the only benefit that Reb Elimelekh conferred on you. In the greatness of his humility, he also caused you to have the merit of giving Reb Elimelekh several gold coins as payment for his sermon."

"BANISH ANGER FROM YOUR MIND"[1]

Once Reb Elimelekh asked his family to prepare his dinner for him early in the evening, since he wanted to go to sleep early that night. They delayed preparing the meal, and in the end it was served to him much later than it usually was. While he was waiting, he kept asking, again and again, and they kept replying that the meal was still not ready.

He said: "Satan is standing over me and is tempting me, saying: 'Elimelekh, why are you keeping quiet? You would be justified in getting angry and shouting at your family to rebuke them.' And he almost made me lose control of myself. But I took counsel with myself and said to him: 'You are evil! Why do you want to drive me out of the world? I wanted to go to sleep early so I could get up early and do the will of my Creator. Now if I go down to the gutter of anger, Heaven forbid, I will transgress His will.' Be at rest once again, O my soul."[2]

RULES TO LIVE BY

Reb Elimelekh said that one should conduct his life according to these guidelines:

One should study Gemara with the commentaries of Rashi, *Tosafot,* and the *poskim* (halakhic authorities) following them, each person according to his ability. First one should study the *Shulhan Arukh,*[3] section 1, *Oraḥ Ḥayyim.*[4] One should request from the Blessed One that he reach the knowledge of the truth.

One should repent deeply for one's sins and should spend time alone before sunrise, which is a propitious time to mourn the exile of the Shekhina (Divine Presence), and should cry with tears. Sometimes also during the day one should be alone; in that way he will remember the sins and transgressions which he had not remembered committing,

1. Eccl. 11:10.
2. Ps. 116:7.
3. Code of Jewish Law of Rabbi Yosef Karo.
4. Covering laws of prayer and synagogue, Shabbat and festivals.

and they will appear to him as hills and mountains. One should do this not once, not twice, but many times, until Heaven will have mercy on him, and one should pray to the Blessed One that He will lead him on the right path so that he does not waste his life.

One should guard oneself against flattery, lies, buffoonery, gossip, jealousy, hatred, competitiveness, anger, and pride.

And one should always keep in mind the day of one's death, and pray to the Blessed One that one should study Torah for its own sake.

One should learn in awe and fear the books of *musar* every day.

And occasionally he should study with awe the writings of Rabbi Yitzḥak Luria, the Arizal, and all of this with awe and fear of the Blessed One.

One must purify one's body and soul with the study of the Gemara and *Tosafot,* and also stories of Aggada in the Gemara, which are very suitable for purifying one's soul.

One should guard oneself from transgressions and from evil thoughts under all circumstances.

One should guard oneself from hating any Jew, except for those one knows for sure are evil, whom it is impossible to judge in the scale of merit, and all whom it is possible to judge in the scale of merit, one must love them as himself with all his soul and might, to fulfill "You shall love your neighbor as yourself."

One should not instill fear in one's family, and one should not be angry in one's home, and if there arise any anger toward anyone regarding something, one should remember immediately the sins of one's youth, and one should tell oneself that this is nothing but his own sins which brought him to this anger. And one should pray to the Blessed One that He should help him to do full repentance, and that one should not die without repenting.

One's words with others should be gentle, and if others praise him he should be sad about it. He should find a quiet corner and ask himself, Why do they praise me for things I do not merit, since if they would know my weaknesses and my foolishness and my evil deeds, how could I show my face before the Blessed Creator, who knows and sees my deeds at all times, and nevertheless He has mercy on me?

Mitzva and Transgression

I AM THE GUILTY ONE

Once Reb Elimelekh asked his son, "Do you know, my son, why such large numbers of people come to me every day and ask me to help them find health and sustenance?

"It is because they probably know that I am responsible for their bad situation. Our sages say that every person must imagine that the world is in a half-and-half situation, and that he is able by his deeds to tilt the scale toward good or to evil. If he does a mitzva he tilts the scale toward merit; if he commits a sin he tilts the scale toward guilt. And they think that because of my sins I tilted the world toward guilt."

GREATER AND LESSER SINS

It happened once that Rav Moshe, the son of the Maggid of Kozhnitz, was a guest at the home of Reb Elimelekh and heard him say about himself that he was more evil than anyone.

Rav Moshe asked, "How can his honor say this? Is he suspected, Heaven forbid, of some terrible transgression?"

Reb Elimelekh replied: "No, but I am suspected of transgressions that are lighter than the terrible ones. However, when one inserts a thin needle into the flesh the pain is much greater than when one is hit with a heavy stick."

EVERY JEW IS FILLED WITH MITZVOT AS A POMEGRANATE IS FILLED WITH SEEDS

Reb Zusha said: "It is stated in tractate Avot, 'Whoever commits one transgression acquires for oneself an accuser.'[1] For every transgression a prosecuting angel is born in the hereafter. Although Zusha never saw an evil Jew in his lifetime, he did see evil angels, angels of destruction, who are created from the transgressions that a Jewish person commits. And I can testify: I have never seen an angel who is totally evil, healthy, and complete in all his limbs. All these angels of destruction are imperfect; one is missing a hand, another missing a foot. For when a Jew commits a transgression, he does not carry it out completely. His evil urge pushes him, but his heart smites him; and from this sin, which no one commits with a full heart, an imperfect angel must be created."

BEAUTIFICATION OF A MITZVA

The Maggid of Mezritch asked one of his students, Rabbi Shneur Zalman, to design new letters for Torah scrolls, tefillin, and mezuzot. He instructed him to make the letters beautiful and in accordance with the halakhic prescriptions of the great *poskim*, as well with the Kabbala.

Rabbi Schneur Zalman sat for a long time, researched and studied, and prepared new shapes of letters, the likes of which had never been seen before. When he finished his work, he parted from his teacher and traveled home by way of the city of Anipoli, the residence of Reb Zusha and Rabbi Moshe Sofer. On the night that he entered the city he knocked on Rabbi Moshe's door, but no one answered. After waiting several minutes, he decided to let himself in, and when he entered the house he found Rabbi Moshe busy writing tefillin, and he stood behind him until he finished a *parasha* (section).

Rabbi Moshe asked forgiveness from his distinguished guest for the delay in opening the door. He had been writing the holy name, he explained, and was not able to pause.

The guest glanced at the letters written by Rabbi Moshe and saw that they resembled exactly the new letters he had designed at the request of the Maggid. He asked Rabbi Moshe where the idea for these

1. Avot 4:11.

letters came from, and Rabbi Moshe replied: "Several days ago Reb Zusha came to me and asked me to write for him several *parashot* (sections) according to the style of letters which he had been shown from heaven the night before."

When this story was told to Rabbi Yosef Yitzḥak, the *Admor* (hasidic spiritual leader) of Lubavitch, he related: "This story I already heard from my holy masters in my youth. At that time they told me that after fifty-six years I would hear this story again. And this year is the fifty-sixth year since the first time I heard it."

"THE REWARD OF A MITZVA IS A MITZVA"[2]

Reb Zusha was extremely poor his whole life. When his daughter reached maturity, Reb Zusha came to his master and told him his troubles: since he had so little money it was difficult for him to marry off his daughter. Whenever a suggestion for a match was made for his daughter, and they heard that he had no money to contribute toward even a small part of the necessary expenses, every suggestion would fade, one after another.

His master took pity on him and made him a generous gift of ten thousand rubles to fulfill the mitzva of *hakhnasat kallah* (assistance to a bride). Reb Zusha left his master with a cheerful and joyous heart.

On his way home he heard weeping coming from the house next door. Reb Zusha went to the house and found a widow crying bitterly. When he asked what happened to her and if he could help, the widow told him that because that evening she was supposed to bring her daughter to the *ḥuppa* to be married, she decided the night before to go to the market to buy her daughter bedding and furniture, as she had promised to her future in-laws. But in the turmoil of the marketplace, to her great sorrow, she lost her purse, which contained all her money. She immediately approached her in-laws and told them what had happened to her, but they suspected that she wanted to shirk her financial obligations and was using the loss of the money as an excuse. Thus the wedding was canceled. Having told her story, the widow again burst out weeping bitterly.

2. Ibid. 4:2.

Reb Zusha asked her, "How much money did you lose?"

She replied: "Ten thousand rubles."

"Did you have any personal marks on the purse of money that was lost?

"Yes, one bundle of rubles was bound with a rubber band and held five thousand rubles, and five additional bundles each had one thousand rubles."

Reb Zusha said to her: "This morning, on my way to the market, I found to my great surprise a bundle of money. Wait a minute, I'll go home and check the details you mentioned, and see if what I found is the money you lost."

The widow did not believe her ears! She was totally focused on the results of the search, hoping that the money he found would turn out to be hers.

After a short while Reb Zusha returned and said to her: "From Heaven salvation has come to you. I checked and found that God brought me the bundle of money that you lost – so here it is!"

When the family counted the money Reb Zusha gave them, they were surprised to see that the package contained a total of only nine thousand rubles.

"So where are the other thousand rubles?" they asked.

"This amount I kept for myself as payment for my efforts," he answered.

Those present were dismayed and demanded that he act morally. Since when do we learn that payment for effort is taken for the mitzva of returning a lost article? they wondered.

Reb Zusha gave his opinion: "The extra money belongs to me legally." The members of the widow's household began to grumble, even to shout: "Please return immediately the balance of one thousand rubles, and if not, we will be forced to take it from you by force, and with a beating!"

Reb Zusha acceded to their request and gave them the package of extra money, which totaled a thousand rubles.

After telling the story to the neighbors, the widow's family went to Reb Zusha's teacher and said to him: "You have a follower, but he is a foolish man," and they told him the whole story.

After hearing the story, Reb Zusha's teacher responded: "You must approach Reb Zusha and ask his forgiveness. You should know that he never found any lost object, and the package of money that he gave you was his own money. This is the money that I myself gave him so he could marry off his daughter."

"If this is really what happened, why did he keep a thousand rubles, which we received from him only after pleas and threats?"

"This you will have to ask Zusha himself," replied the rabbi.

The neighbors rushed to the scantily furnished home of Reb Zusha to clarify exactly what was the truth.

Zusha said to them, "The rabbi is right. That's exactly what happened. When I went to my house and heard crying coming from the widow's house, and when it became clear to me that the wedding of her daughter, which was set for that evening, had been canceled, I felt sorry for her and immediately I decided to donate to her the same money that the rabbi gave me to marry off my daughter. However, so that the widow would not be shamed that she needs a free gift, I asked her for signs that were on her purse, and I added that I would go home and examine the packet of money I had 'found' in order to see if the signs that she specified matched. All this I did so that the widow would be confident and convinced that the money which I would give her was really hers.

"I waited a while and then returned to the house of the widow to transfer the 'lost' money to her. While walking there, I realized that I was guilty of taking pride in the fact that the Blessed Holy One had given me the privilege of fulfilling the mitzva of *hashavat aveda* (returning a lost article). I was saying to myself: Zusha, your reward in the next world is assured, since you are fulfilling the mitzva of gladdening the heart of a widow. So then I said to myself: Zusha, is this the way to fulfill mitzvot? You are not fulfilling a mitzva for its own sake! Are you not worried about the verse 'Every haughty person is an abomination to the Lord'?[3]

"Therefore I decided that I must hold back a thousand rubles under the pretext of receiving a payment for my efforts, and for that I

3. Prov. 16:5.

would surely receive words of mockery, anger, and contempt, and then I would hand over to the widow the other thousand rubles. In this way I would have performed a full mitzva, since we learned that the reward of a mitzva is a mitzva, with no expectation of reward or payment, either in this world or the next."

Prayer

THEIR MOTHER'S BLESSINGS

Mirl, the mother of Reb Elimelekh and Reb Zusha, could not read the prayer book and knew no prayers except the morning blessings. But Reb Zusha used to say that on the place where she had stood to say the blessings, the holy Shekhina would rest throughout the day.

HE IS MINE

When a true Hasid pours out his heart before his Maker and prays, "Grant me wisdom, understanding, and knowledge," his intention is not that the Creator should grant him the wisdom of logical thought, the understanding of convincing logic, and the knowledge that develops the intellect. At the hour of prayer he intends that God should open before him the gate of understanding, that He lift a bit the curtain that covers the universe, that He open his inner eye in order to be able to see more, feel more, in the sense of "Open my eyes that I may see the wonders of Your Torah."[1]

Rabbi Yitzḥak Eizik of Komarno relates that one day after prayer, Reb Elimelekh turned to one of his students and poured out the bitterness in his heart: "I prayed today with the deepest fervor, without causing myself any distraction from the meaning of the prayer. I even ventured from one upper world to the next without any delay or interruption. This

1. Ps. 119:18.

must be only because the evil inclination, Satan, came to this conclusion, saying: 'Why should I disturb Elimelekh while he prays with fervor and devotion, and why should I delay him from climbing from world to world? Indeed in any case all his deeds are not for Heaven's sake, and therefore he is completely mine and he and also his prayers are mine!'"

Here Reb Elimelekh burst into bitter tears and cried: "It seems to me therefore that I am already lost from both worlds together!"

WILL GOD RESTORE MY SOUL?

Reb Elimelekh would say: "I am late in reciting my prayers, because it is not possible for me to get myself ready earlier. You say I should arise early in the morning to prepare myself at the right time? I cannot because I am also late going to sleep. You ask why do I not go to sleep on time? I will answer you: I cannot go to sleep on time, because when it is my turn to sleep I am doing an accounting of my soul, and I am very much afraid to go to sleep, since who knows if I will merit that God will return my soul again.

"Therefore I am afraid of going to sleep and because of this I go to bed late every night. But against my will I lie down in order to snooze a bit, and the next morning I am late in reciting my prayers."

THE VEIN

The grandson of Rabbi Yisrael Baal Shem Tov, Rabbi Moshe Ephraim, author of *Degel Maḥaneh Ephraim,* was not happy with the Polish Hasidim because he had heard that they afflicted themselves excessively and destroyed their "image of God" instead of improving their body and blending it with the soul to make it a holy vessel to serve the Creator.

After the death of Reb Elimelekh, his favorite student, Rabbi Mendel of Rimanov, went to Rabbi Moshe Ephraim to ask him, as the deceased had ordered, about taking Reb Elimelekh's place.

Rabbi Moshe Ephraim knew that he was a Polish Hasid, and received him with coolness. Rabbi Mendel's countenance changed out of sorrow.

Rabbi Moshe Ephraim looked at him attentively. His forehead, which had paled, and his wide open eyes testified that he was not a simple man but a person of substance. Rabbi Moshe Ephraim asked him pleasantly, "Have you traveled to see the tzaddik yet?"

"I served my teacher and my esteemed rabbi, Reb Elimelekh," answered Rabbi Mendel,

Immediately Rabbi Moshe Ephraim looked at Rabbi Mendel with admiration, and again asked: "What is the most wonderful thing that you saw about this marvelous man?" With this question he thought to himself: Now this Hasid with a shining face will reveal his true character and will tell me some story of miracles.

Rabbi Mendel answered him: "Every day when our teacher was deeply meditating on the awesome majesty of the Blessed One, his whole body shook with fear and his face paled. And I learned from my teacher that beneath a man's ear there is one vein which does not move at all unless he is about to die, and as my teacher and my master, Reb Elimelekh was praying, even this vein was pulsing out of fear and awe."

Rabbi Moshe Ephraim was silent. After a while he said: "I did not know that," and then he said again: "I did not know that," and accepted Rabbi Mendel with open arms.

THE STOVE LIGHTER

When Reb Zusha was already close to the Maggid of Mezritch and conducted himself as a complete Hasid in all matters, his brother Reb Elimelekh was still a *mitnaged* (opponent of Hasidism). Reb Zusha would pray a lot and spend many hours in the company of the students of the Maggid, listening to new hasidic insights and miracle stories and even singing and dancing with them. Reb Elimelekh, as was the custom of *mitnagdim,* spent much time studying Torah, being alone in his room, and distancing himself from friendly conversation.

Once Reb Elimelekh asked Reb Zusha: "Zusha, why do you neglect Torah study and occupy yourself always with prayer and singing and discussions with Hasidim?"

Reb Zusha told this story: "A certain woodcutter deeply desired to be among those who were close to the king. What did he do? He left the village of his birth and became a wanderer. For many years he wandered from city to city and from village to village, until he came to the capital. Once there he approached the gate of the palace and stood there many days without moving from his place. He thought that probably the king came and went through that gate, and thus he would have an opportunity to see him face-to-face.

"The guard at the gate saw him and asked him what he wanted. Mumbling and embarrassed, the woodcutter told him. The guard, seeing that he was a simple man, had mercy on him and brought him inside to the official in charge of the court facing the palace. The woodcutter, in his innocence, found favor in the eyes of the official in charge of the court, who brought him to the official in charge of the palace.

"Finally they permitted the woodcutter to come every day to the court of the king and light the stoves in the rooms of all the officials who lived there. He did his work faithfully and was diligent in lighting the stoves in the proper way.

"When the king heard that the stoves were working well, which was not so before, he summoned the stove lighter and said to him, 'Since I have found you to be an honest and upright man who does his work faithfully, tell me what you desire and I will fulfill it.'

"The stove lighter said to him, 'I have only one wish: to enjoy the glorious majesty of the king. My only request is that the king command that I be given a small room with a window, so that I can stand there always and look outside. And when the king passes by there, I will merit to look upon his shining figure.' The king ordered that this be done.

"It happened once that the prince sinned against his father and was sentenced to be banished from his father's palace for a whole year. The prince roamed around the court, sad and gloomy. He came to the stove lighter and asked him to give him his clothing and let him stand in his place near the window, to look at the face of his father the king when he passed by, since he longed to see him.

"The stove lighter said to him: 'It is not proper for you to stand in my place to see the king's face. You are his son, and surely it is right for you to be among those who see him always. You only have to ask forgiveness from your father and to promise that from now on you will behave with intelligence and reason. It is not the same for me. Who am I? If I do not stand in my place and do my job, I will never merit to see the king's face.'

"My brother Elimelekh, your great strength is in Torah, and you are a member of the household of our Father the King in heaven. But I am simple Zusha, a boor and ignoramus; I will never merit to reach the king's court if I do not pray with enthusiasm and light the stove of the Master of the Universe."

WHISPER OR SHOUT?

There is a tzaddik who can work and pray in a whisper,
His every statement makes an impression,
And there is a tzaddik who is not on that level,
He needs to pray in a shout to the Blessed One.

– Reb Elimelekh of Lizhensk

SWEETER THAN HONEY

Reb Elimelekh said:
There are tzaddikim who cannot chant a *niggun*,
And nevertheless when they pray their voice is pleasant
And sweeter than nectar and honey.

– Reb Elimelekh of Lizhensk

Rabbi and Student

HE SEARCHES HEARTS

When Rabbi Shmelke and Rabbi Pinḥas, two brothers who were distinguished scholars, came to Rabbi Dov Ber, the Maggid of Mezritch, for the first time, they were not impressed at all with their reception. Immediately they got up and left him to return to their city, since they were afraid that to stay there would involve *bittul Torah* (neglect of Torah study).

As they were leaving, the Maggid suggested to them that they have a brief discussion with Zusha, who lit the stove in his house. They sat for a while with Zusha and again got up to leave.

As they were leaving, Zusha began to interpret for them the verse "If a man enters a hiding place, do I not see him? says the Lord."[1] He said: "If a man is concealed in a hiding place in his room for the purpose of *hitbodedut* (solitude, being alone with God) and to study Torah and service of the Creator, but he says 'and I,' remembering his 'I' – then 'Do I not see him, says the Lord'; in other words, the Blessed One says: I do not want to see him and am distancing Myself from him."

Reb Zusha's words entered their hearts and aroused in them submission and a truly broken heart. Zusha looked at them and said: "And again one can interpret this verse as follows. 'If a man enters a hiding place, do I not' – namely, he forgets the 'I' since he has attained the realization

1. Jer. 23:24.

that the 'I' is nothing – then 'I will see him, says the Lord'; in other words, the Blessed One says: I will see him favorably and I will bring him to Me."

The two brothers, who were distinguished scholars, saw that Zusha searched hearts and knew their thoughts.

WHO IS WISE? ONE WHO LEARNS FROM EVERYONE[2]

Before he became famous as Reb Zusha of Anipoli, Zusha stood out among the students of the Maggid of Mezritch.

He was not a genius and was not counted among the Torah greats; he was not a brilliant scholar in debates; he never wrote books or composed responsa and halakhic decisions. But he was a tzaddik, pious and humble, and he loved his people with a boundless love. Because of this he was privileged to have his people praise him for the many legends that they could weave around him.

He would visit the home of his teacher, the Maggid of Mezritch, twice each year: before Pesach and during the month of Elul. Each time he would tarry there three months, study the ways of Hasidism with his teacher and his outstanding pupils, and absorb holiness and purity.

One year on the afternoon of Rosh Ḥodesh Nisan, he went to Mezritch and came into the home of the Maggid to greet him. The Maggid was partaking of a festive Rosh Ḥodesh meal together with his students. After the meal was finished, he greeted Reb Zusha and said to him: "Zusha, my son, I order you to return home today and celebrate Pesach with your family."

"My master," pleaded Reb Zusha, "have I not come to spend two or three months to learn the ways of the tzaddikim? Naturally, I am prepared to withdraw my desire in favor of your will, but before I leave my master, I would like to receive from him some instructions in the ways of service and the paths of Hasidism."

"Excellent," replied the Maggid. "'Who is wise? One who learns from everyone,' even from an infant or a thief.

"Three things we learn from an infant: An infant is constantly enveloped in joy, and sadness cannot rule him. An infant is never idle for even a minute. When an infant wants something from his father, anything, he only asks with tears.

2. Avot 4:1.

"And seven things we learn from a thief: The essence of the work of a thief is at night. If a thief does not succeed one night, he does not despair but tests his powers the next night. A thief loves his friends as himself, and each is prepared to give his life for his friend. A thief is ready to risk his life for even the least important matter, and even if it is doubtful. A thief's work is not worth anything to him, and the next morning he sells what he stole at night for a minimal price. When a thief takes a beating, he accepts punishment for disobedience and stands and screams: I do not know. A thief loves his profession and would not trade it for anything in the world."

These ten teachings, which he heard from his great master, were etched in Reb Zusha's mind, and in accordance with them he directed all his deeds.

I UNDERSTOOD WHAT WAS MEANT BY THE WORDS

Reb Zusha would say: "When I first saw the face of my master, my teacher, the Maggid of Mezritch, I understood what was meant by the words of our sages: 'Let the reverence you have for your teacher be like the reverence due to Heaven.'[3] At that moment all the hair on my head fell out from reverence and fear of Hashem and the glory of His majesty."

GET YOURSELF A TEACHER[4]

Among the Hasidim of Reb Zusha of Anipoli was a wealthy man who from time to time would come to visit him and bring him a special present. One day he came and did not find the rabbi at home.

"Where is the rabbi?" he asked Reb Zusha's wife.

"The rabbi," she answered, "went to his rabbi."

"What?" said the rich man. "Even the rabbi himself has a rabbi?"

"Yes," said the rabbi's wife, "his rabbi is the Maggid of Mezritch."

When the rich man heard about this he reasoned: If through my travels to my rabbi I have succeeded in my business, how much more will I succeed if I travel to my rabbi's rabbi?

---

3. Ibid. 1:6.
4. Ibid. 4:12.

So from that time he began to travel to the Maggid of Mezritch. But the more he traveled there, the more his success left him. He began to examine his actions, and he realized that he was being punished for offending the honor of Reb Zusha when he stopped traveling to him. He therefore went to Anipoli, and when he met with the rabbi he conciliated him and asked: "May my teacher please forgive me and explain to me: Why is it that when I visited him I was successful, thank God, and my success increased more and more. But when I began to travel to the rabbi of Mezritch, to whom even the honorable rabbi goes, my success was taken from me all at once?"

"The matter is simple," said Reb Zusha to him. "Truth to tell, I myself am not a tzaddik at all. I am a simple Jew like all Jews, and so all the time that you came to me and gave me money, even though I did not deserve it, you were not scrutinized in heaven and they gave you much, even though perhaps you did not deserve it. But from the time that you began to scrutinize and ask for privileges, and to find for yourself a true tzaddik, the Maggid of Mezritch, they began to scrutinize you in heaven, and therefore your success was diminished."

SERVING SCHOLARS

Once when Rabbi Ḥayyim of Czernowitz, author of *Be'er Mayim Ḥayyim,* was staying with Reb Elimelekh, Reb Zusha said to Rabbi Ḥayyim: "I examined my soul and I find that Zusha is going to destruction. Zusha succeeds at nothing, not at Torah, not at fear of Heaven. There is no remedy for Zusha. There is nothing left for Zusha except to serve scholars in a physical way. I request from your honor, Rabbi Ḥayyim, that you grant me the merit to perform this mitzva – to serve a great scholar such as you, and since on the path from the beit midrash to your inn there is a lot of mud, I am prepared to lie down in the mud under your feet, and you can pass over me. It is possible that in this way there will be a remedy for my sinful soul."

PEOPLE OF GOOD LINEAGE

Rabbi Naftali of Ropshitz came frequently to learn from Reb Elimelekh but Reb Elimelekh did not want to accept him as a student. He said, "I do not want privileged students."

Rabbi Naftali wept and pleaded before him, prostrating himself on the ground and crying bitterly. "What is my sin that my father was well born?" he argued.

Reb Elimelekh had compassion on him, brought him close to him, and treated him with great affection.

THE POWER OF SPEECH

Rabbi Yisrael of Ruzhin told this story: "All the students of my grandfather, the Maggid of Mezritch, taught Torah in his name, except for Reb Zusha, and the reason was that anytime the Maggid spoke, Reb Zusha didn't listen until he had finished. For at the beginning of his remarks, when the Maggid pronounced the verse from the Torah in order to comment upon it, and began reading the verse, saying, 'And God said,' or 'And God spoke,' immediately Reb Zusha would cry out and shake so hard that he disturbed everyone sitting nearby and they had to remove him. So he would stand in the corridor or in the woodshed, bang on the walls, and shout: 'And God said,' and he would not quiet down until the Maggid stopped speaking. But the truth is, if the tzaddik speaks the truth, and the one who receives it, receives it in truth, one word is enough. With one word it is possible to bring near the whole world; with one word it is possible to purify the whole world."

A FRIEND LIKE A BROTHER

A very strong bond existed between Reb Elimelekh and his beloved friend from the beit midrash of the Maggid of Mezritch, the defender of Israel, Rabbi Levi Yitzḥak of Berdichev.

Reb Elimelekh admired Rabbi Levi Yitzḥak limitlessly and praised in great measure his piety, his glowing prayers, and his enormous strength in defending the Jewish people. He would say: "Even while he is sleeping Rabbi Levi Yitzḥak's heart trembles inside him from an abundance of fear and awe before the Blessed Holy One, not less than a man walking in the forest who finds himself suddenly surrounded by a band of robbers on all sides."

Further, he said: "Every morning a proclamation goes forth in the Upper Worlds announcing: 'Prepare to welcome Rabbi Levi Yitzḥak of Berdichev, who is soon to arrive with two wagons loaded with mitzvot and good deeds of holy Jews, ready to plead their cause and defend them, and to cancel all types of accusations.'"

A SPIRITUAL INHERITANCE

Before his death Reb Elimelekh placed his hand on his four students, one after another, and gave them gifts. To Rabbi Yaakov Yitzḥak, the Seer of Lublin, he gave the light of his eyes; to Rabbi Avraham Yehoshua Heschel of Apta he gave his power of speech; to Rabbi Yisrael of Kozhnitz he gave his power of prayer; and to Rabbi Mendel of Rimanov he gave his intelligence.

The Scale of Merit

THE SCALE OF MERIT

The people are right, who come to me and cry out:
"Give us children, life, and sustenance."
The world is always half innocent and half guilty,
And I, in my sins, tipped the scales of the world to the side of guilt.
This is the reason for poverty, this is the reason for suffering.
It is fitting, therefore, that I be accountable,
And it is fitting that people make a claim against me for their suffering.

– Reb Elimelekh of Lizhensk

WORDS OF ACCUSATION AND REBUKE DELAY THE REDEMPTION

Rabbi Aryeh Leib, the Rebuker of Polnoye, was one of the great *maggidim* in eastern Europe in the eighteenth century. As one of the students of the holy Baal Shem Tov, he influenced many people, both scholars and simple folk, to join the hasidic movement.

It happened once that Rabbi Aryeh Leib of Polnoye and Reb Zusha of Anipoli were together during a visit to the tzaddik Rabbi Aryeh Leib of Shpoli, the Saba of Shpoli.

Reb Zusha arose and said to Rabbi Aryeh Leib of Polnoye in a resentful tone: "With all due respect, Rabbi Leib, you carry on your shoulders a heavy burden of guilt for the delay of the coming of the

Messiah. You travel around to the communities of Jews and speak with accusations and rebuke toward the brothers and sisters of our people. If you would only speak positively to them, your words would hasten the coming of the Messiah."

Rabbi Aryeh Leib was perturbed by the piercing words of Reb Zusha and did not rush to reply to them. The Saba of Shpoli said to his distinguished guests: "Indeed, there is a strong foundation to the words of Reb Zusha: I too think that the Jewish people do not return to their good ways through rebukes and punishments, but rather from 'the abundance of everything,' as it is written in *Parashat Ki Tavo:* 'Because you would not serve the Lord your God in joy and gladness over the abundance of everything.'[1] We learn from the words of the Torah that with 'the abundance of everything' it is more comfortable and easier to serve God."

THE WHOLE COMMUNITY SHALL BE FORGIVEN FOR IT HAPPENED THROUGH ERROR[2]

During the days of his wandering Reb Elimelekh of Lizhensk, dressed as a beggar, came into a tavern and entered the kitchen to wash his hands. A piece of bread was removed from the oven, and a loaf of bread was stolen. Suspicion fell on the beggar, who meanwhile had left, and they sent the servant after him. The servant caught him and slapped his face with no discussion. Reb Elimelekh accepted the slaps submissively.

Suddenly a fire broke out in the tavern. The owners suspected that perhaps the fire was a punishment for the injustice that the beggar had suffered. The owner of the tavern quickly rode on his horse to find the beggar and appease him. When he found him he begged forgiveness.

But Reb Elimelekh paid no attention to the request and did not even look at the man who requested forgiveness, since his eyes were lifted to Heaven as he whispered these words:

"Master of the Universe, please forgive Elimelekh, since due to his shame a fire was caused in a Jewish home. Elimelekh deserved this disgrace. And You, Master of the Universe, have mercy on this Jew and direct that the fire in his house be extinguished immediately."

---

1. Deut. 28:47.
2. Num. 15:26.

SIGHING IN SILENCE

It happened that once during their wanderings Reb Zusha and Reb Elimelekh stayed overnight in a certain village. That very same night two horses were stolen from the village tax collector. The tax collector immediately suspected that the two vagabonds, whose faces and dress resembled that of beggars, had "appropriated" the horses. He chased and caught them and immediately began to beat them. Since they did not struggle with him but accepted the heavy blows in silence and submission, it seemed certain that they were involved in the act of thievery. He continued to beat them severely without any investigation or inquiry. Only at the end, when he broke out in an angry rebuke, shouting, "Thieves, give me back the horses," did the two brothers stare at him in astonishment. At that moment the moon came out from behind the clouds, and one look at their faces made it clear to the tax collector that they were blameless.

When the tax collector saw this, he again rebuked them angrily: "All right, you are not thieves, but your beating was deserved. When Jews are beaten and do not scream or say a single word, it is obvious that they know they deserve a good beating."

The tax collector left them to themselves. At that moment Reb Zusha said: "It is true, Elimelekh, that it was fitting for us to receive this beating, and even more, in order to learn this inference: Consider the punishment of sinners! If we, who were only suspected of thievery, deserved such a beating, how much more must thieves, who are not only suspected but who really occupy themselves with thievery, be beaten. Mercy on them!"

JUSTIFYING THE MAJORITY

Once Reb Zusha of Anipoli saw a Jew steal a loaf of bread and devour it without washing his hands or saying the blessing. Reb Zusha said: "I thank you, Lord my God, that You gave this Jew such a hearty appetite that he could not hold back from eating before washing his hands. Zusha doesn't have an appetite like that. He eats only a little and is therefore ill and weak. Zusha is not a good Jew. A Jew must be healthy, at least as much as a non-Jew. And doesn't the Rambam teach, 'If the body is healthy it is because of God'?[3] And this is the secret of the Talmudic saying on the

3. *Hilkhot Deot* 4:1.

verse 'And you shall love the Lord your God with all your heart':[4] with both of your urges, with the good urge and with the evil urge."[5]

Reb Zusha was accustomed, like Rabbi Levi Yitzḥak of Berdichev, to be an advocate for Israel. It happened once before shofar blowing that Reb Zusha left his beit midrash and met a Jewish child from among the poor, wearing torn, ragged clothing.

"My son," asked Reb Zusha, "are you not jealous of the non-Jewish children who eat their fill and wear fancy clothing?"

"No," replied the child, "I am not jealous of them at all. I am a Jew and I fear the Lord of heaven, and I am happy with my lot."

Reb Zusha returned to the beit midrash, opened the holy ark, and said: "Lord of the Universe, look down from heaven and see who are like Your people Israel. A Jewish child, even when he is hungry and thirsty, and dressed in rags, accepts everything with love and is happy and proud of his Jewishness."

It happened once that Reb Zusha placed several currency notes inside a *Ḥumash,* in *Parashat Yitro,* where it is written, "Thou shalt not steal." When he left his room, someone came in who was learned in the laws of *netilat yadayim* (ritual hand washing)[6] and removed one note from the *Ḥumash* and put the rest of them in *Parashat Kedoshim* at the verse "And you shall love your neighbor as yourself."

When Reb Zusha returned to his room and saw what had happened, he called out: "Master of the Universe, look down from heaven and see Your people Israel, the holy children of holy parents, how righteous they are! This person surely is very needy and by rights he should take all the money, but he did not want to transgress 'Thou shalt not steal,' and took only what he needed. And the rest of the money he left in place to fulfill 'Love your neighbor as yourself.' Therefore, God, give to the people of Israel an abundance of livelihood, blessing, and success, that Your people the House of Israel should never need to take from one another nor from another people."

4. Deut. 6:5.
5. Berakhot 54a.
6. This is a play on words: *netilat yadayim* can also be read in this context as "taking with the hands."

Service of the Creator

KEYS TO THE HEART

After the death of Reb Elimelekh of Lizhensk, his students sought for themselves a tzaddik to replace him. They came to visit the Seer of Lublin, but when they saw that the Seer's path in divine service was not the path they were accustomed to with their rabbi in Lizhensk, they decided to leave Lublin to search for another tzaddik.

When they went into the private room of the Seer to receive a parting blessing, he said to them: "The Torah has seventy faces, but regarding the service of God there are four hundred paths. What value is there to God, as it were, if there is only one path to serve Him? Our teacher the holy Besht taught us that God wants us to serve Him in all the different ways, but that path one must choose with all one's might.

"There is a long corridor which leads to the inner living room in which the Creator dwells, and there are many gates carved in the corridor. The corridor is open to all, but each gate is opened with a key that fits the qualities of the person who crosses the threshold. There is a gate which is opened through joy, and there is a gate which only tears can open. There is a gate which is opened by the strength of praise and appreciation, and there is a gate opened by prayer and confession. There is a gate which is opened by love, and one that is opened by fear."

And the tzaddik imposed on his students the obligation to search for the path to which each person is inclined – "but that path one must choose with all one's might."

HOW DOES ONE SERVE GOD?

A Hasid came to Reb Zusha of Anipoli and asked: "How do we serve the Blessed One?"

Reb Zusha replied: "Do I serve God that I should know how we should serve Him? I mingle among Hasidim, and from them I heard: Just as we make our beds, so we sleep. Just as we sleep, so we get up, and just as we get up, so do we awaken, and just as we awaken, so do we serve God."

THE WAYS OF TZADDIKIM IN SERVING THE CREATOR

The tzaddik Rabbi Shmuel Shmelke HaLevi Horowitz of Nikolsburg was accustomed to sleep just a few hours each night. He would lean on his table and hold a burning candle between his fingers. He did this so that he would awaken when the candle burned down and its flame reached his fingertips.

It happened once that Reb Elimelekh visited him, and after a long conversation he thought to convince Rabbi Shmuel Shmelke to lie down to sleep, as all people do, without grasping the candle during his nap. When the tzaddik fell asleep in his bed, Reb Elimelekh closed the window in the room and covered his host with a warm blanket. Thus Rabbi Shmuel Shmelke had a long and pleasant sleep.

When he awakened from his sleep the next morning, Rabbi Shmuel Shmelke felt that his mind was very clear. "Now," he said to his guest, "it is obvious to me that even by sleeping in my bed it is possible to serve the Creator."

THE TOMBSTONE

On the tombstone of Reb Zusha these words are inscribed:
"He served God out of love, and rejoiced in hardship,
And he brought many back from sin."

Soul

A HOLY SPARK

There is no creation in the world
That does not have a holy spark
Which gives it its vitality.
And were it not for its holy spark
It could not survive.

– Reb Elimelekh of Lizhensk

DOUBTS OF HERESY IN THE HEART

Reb Elimelekh once asked Reb Zusha: "In one of the books of the Kabbala there is a statement that all of the souls of every generation were included in the soul of *Adam HaRishon* (the first man). If this is so, I am surprised at you, Zusha, my dear brother. You have a pure and holy soul, which was also included in the soul of *Adam HaRishon,* so why did you permit him to transgress the command of God and eat from the Tree of Knowledge?"

"My dear brother," answered Reb Zusha in innocence, "if my soul had prevented him from eating from the Tree of Knowledge, would not Adam have remained full of doubts and thoughts of heresy? He would always have wondered if maybe the snake was really right when it said, 'But God knows that as soon as you eat of it your eyes will be opened and you will be like divine beings.'[1] And surely you know what our sages said: 'Thoughts of transgression are worse than transgression itself.'[2] And so both my soul and yours agreed, my brother, that he should sin by eating from the Tree of Knowledge so that he would realize that the snake is a liar and a fraud, and evil ideas and strange thoughts would not nibble away at his heart and confuse his mind."

THE ROCK FROM WHICH IT WAS HEWN

Reb Elimelekh was talking with his students about the secret of yearnings that seize a person at a time of heavenly mercy. He said to them: "The soul of a mortal prior to its descent to our world is led by an angel through all the worlds. And at the moment before it departs from the treasury of souls, there flashes before it, for just one minute, the light of Creation which was hidden in the treasury of lights of above after the sin of *Adam HaRishon*. Why? So that the soul, while it dwells in the body of a human, will long for the same light and pine to be close to it."

1. Gen. 3:5.
2. Yoma 29a.

Spirituality and Physicality

"YOU SATISFY EVERY LIVING THING WITH YOUR FAVOR"[1]

It happened once that Reb Elimelekh came to visit his colleague in Besht-style Hasidism, Rabbi Shmuel Shmelke Horowitz, the rabbi of Nikolsburg.

Reb Elimelekh did not favor those who practiced self-mortification. And when he entered the beit midrash of Rabbi Shmuel, he found Rabbi Shmuel's student, Rabbi Mordechai Benet, sitting and studying Torah with awe and reverence. He approached him, looked at him, and saw in his face that he afflicted his body. He rebuked him, saying: "Young man, of you and those like you Scripture says, 'They are clever at doing wrong, but unable to do right.'[2] Return from your evil path and Hashem will be with you."

Rabbi Mordechai was alarmed to hear these most bitter words from the mouth of one of the giants of Hasidism, a friend of his holy rabbi, but he did not find in himself any sin or transgression. He rushed to the home of his teacher, Rabbi Shmuel, and with a broken heart he poured out his pain regarding the words that he had heard from Rabbi Shmuel's guest, the rabbi of Lizhensk.

Rabbi Shmuel replied: "My dear student, you are a tzaddik in all your ways, but you are not a Hasid in all your actions. The obligation of

---

1. Ps. 145:16.
2. Jer. 4:22.

a Hasid is not to torture one's body and separate oneself from life, but to penetrate into the depths of life, to eat and drink and find even within the pleasure of material life spiritual enjoyment and sparks of holiness.

"To our disappointment." continued Rabbi Shmuel, "some are mistaken and think that only through self-affliction and fasting can they purify their body and purge their soul. Concerning these people, as my friend Reb Elimelekh says, Scripture states: 'They are clever at doing wrong, but unable to do right. "And this is according to how Rashi explains the verse in Leviticus: 'When a person utters an oath to bad or good purpose'[3] – to harm oneself or to improve oneself, for example, to eat or not to eat – these people are clever at doing wrong, namely, at afflicting themselves and not eating, but unable to do right, to eat and to drink, to enjoy life and find everywhere spiritual life and sparks of holiness. Such people do not know that they can create an atmosphere of holiness even within material life. To them – and you are counted among them – my friend Reb Elimelekh refers in his words, and you should listen to his teachings and improve your actions."

From then on, say the Hasidim, Rabbi Mordechai stopped his asceticism and his fasting. But nevertheless, throughout his life he contented himself with a very limited diet. The following note was found in his *siddur* (prayer book), in his handwriting: "I hereby promise to God, the Lord of Hosts, that I will not enjoy things of this world other than what is absolutely necessary for my physical health."

I AM HAPPY THAT I AM HUNGRY

Rabbi Moshe Leib of Sassov walked on foot to see Reb Elimelekh of Lizhensk and vowed not to ask for anything from anyone on the way, until someone would have mercy on him by divine providence and would give him a coin to buy a slice of bread. Several days passed, and he met no one who would take pity on him. Weak from hunger and feeling discouraged, he pondered in his heart: Is there a limit to the Lord's power to sustain me on my journey? Then what? Perhaps the Blessed One does not want it so, but if He does not want to sustain me – how can I love Him?

3. Lev. 5:4

Immediately he felt remorse for that alien thought. He searched his heart and said to himself: Is eating so important? Even the lowliest creature worries about its belly and hunts for food. But man is superior to the beast in his ability to place a limit on his appetite, and just as he blesses food, so must he give praise and appreciation to the Blessed One for his hunger. The appetite for eating is a sign that the body is healthy. Many are the kings and nobles whose homes are filled with every good thing and whose tables are overflowing with royal dainties. Do these leaders enjoy paradise on earth? They have all the food they could want, but an appetite to eat it they have not.

But you, Moshe Leib, may God's holy name be blessed, you have the appetite of a dog, of a bear, of a lion! You owe Hashem thousands of thanks that you are hungry as a wolf, as a tiger. Then why are you silent, Moshe Leib? Open your mouth and call out in a loud voice which breaks through the heavens: Thank You, Master of the Universe, for the good gift of hunger that You bestowed upon me. Thank You, my Father in heaven, that I am hungry. And for this too my love for You is marvelous, my Father in heaven!

Rabbi Moshe Leib then raised his voice loudly, and in a voice as powerful as the roar of a lion, he called out: "Thank you, Blessed One, that I am hungry!"

Rabbi Moshe Leib looked this way and that way and saw that he was standing in the midst of a thick forest, with towering trees surrounding him, and an awesome glory over all. His spirit was moved greatly, his feet lifted him in dance, and his mouth opened in song.

Just then a wagon passed near him. The passengers saw a Jew shouting and dancing. "Who are you?" they asked. He replied," I am one of the Hasidim of Reb Elimelekh!" They said, "We too are among the Hasidim of Reb Elimelekh." They invited him to sit in the wagon and gave him a slice of bread, and even something to drink.

When Rabbi Moshe Leib stepped over the threshold of Reb Elimelekh's house, the latter said to him, "Oh, my, Moshe Leib. Because a young man punished himself with a bit of hunger, is it permissible for him to be so spoiled before the Master of the Universe, and to reach even as far as arrogance? No, Moshe Leib, with a little hunger a young man is not yet a man of quality."

IN PLEASANT WAYS

A certain Hasid of Reb Elimelekh conducted himself in the hasidic way in all matters, except for his love of eating. It happened once that Reb Elimelekh invited him to share breakfast with him. The Hasid rejoiced greatly at the opportunity to sit with his rabbi for a meal.

On the table was only a piece of dark bread, salt, and a knife. While the pieces of bread were still in their mouths, Reb Elimelekh said: "Woe to you, Elimelekh. Pay attention to how you are eating, glutton that you are. You can't wait to swallow the bread in one gulp. Even with your eyes you eat. Your appetite for food is even bigger than that of an animal. Elimelekh, Elimelekh, stop it. Be a mensch. Remember that eating is permitted only to preserve your life, so that you will have strength to serve the Creator."

Reb Elimelekh sliced another small piece of bread and said: "Elimelekh, Elimelekh, woe to you, you are only deceiving yourself. You pretend to be willing to defeat your *yetzer hara* (evil inclination). You promised yourself that from now on you would be careful in your eating and eat only for the sake of Heaven, so you would have strength to study, to pray, and to serve the Creator. Look, Elimelekh, what a glutton you are. Your whole body says 'eat.' Your mouth eats, and with all your 248 limbs you are swallowing. And with this you have the nerve to think that you are doing it for the sake of Heaven."

After this Reb Elimelekh began to defend himself a bit, and he said: "Elimelekh really wants to defeat his urge to eat. But he has no choice, Elimelekh, because Elimelekh is only flesh and blood. Against his will he eats. The body requires food. It says: 'If you don't feed me, I will die.' It tells me: 'You are my brother, and you must sustain me.'"

When the Hasid heard the words of his rabbi, he almost fainted from sorrow and shame. From then on he changed his ways of eating and became a Hasid in every way.

APPETITE

Reb Zusha said: "When a guest comes to your home, you can give him food, but you cannot give him a desire to eat. We recite in our prayers,

'He feeds every creature to its heart's content'[4] – and this refers to one's appetite, since an appetite is something only the Blessed Holy One can give."

WHERE TO LIVE

The main place of residence for someone is in the Upper Worlds.

– Reb Elimelekh of Lizhensk

MEALS

The poor person at his meager meal
Is likely to sink into desire
More than the rich man
At his extravagant meal.

– Reb Elimelekh of Lizhensk

SPIRITUAL VERSUS MATERIAL

There is no physicality
That does not have sparks of spirituality.

– Reb Elimelekh of Lizhensk

4. Ps. 145:16.

Sustenance

MAKING A LIVING

"Beware lest your heart grow haughty and you forget the Lord your God" (Deuteronomy 8:14).
Is it possible for a Jew, Heaven forbid, to forget the Lord his God out of an abundance of success?
No, no, no.
If he is distracted for a moment,
It is only because of the weight of the yoke of the exile, and the hardship of making a living.
Master of the Universe, please give sustenance with ease and with honor to Your people Israel,
And they will all unite in one fellowship to do Your will wholeheartedly,[1]
Since they all want to fear Your name.

– Reb Zusha of Anipoli

WE ARE DEPENDENT ON YOU[2]

During most of his life Reb Zusha lived in abject poverty, and his family was often hungry for bread, but he was always filled with joy and never complained about his situation.

1. From the High Holiday prayers.
2. From the Yom Kippur liturgy (*Ne'ila* prayer).

Once one of his relatives came to see him. Reb Zusha's wife began to complain to him about their indigent household, how the children were asking for food and there wasn't any. She could not bear it any longer. From much pain and sorrow she began to cry.

"Where is your husband?" asked the guest.

"He is in the beit midrash all day," answered his wife bitterly.

The guest went to the beit midrash and found Reb Zusha sitting and reciting psalms to a melody, with joy and delight.

"Go home and see!" his relative rebuked him. "Your wife and family are dying of hunger and weeping, and you are happy and singing."

"They are crying, and they have reason to cry," answered Reb Zusha innocently, "since their eyes are turned toward me, to poor Zusha, who has nothing to give them. But my eyes are turned to the Blessed Holy One, so should I not rejoice?"

Once several people in his city rebuked him for not worrying about supporting his family. They reminded him of the teaching: "One who gives *tzedaka* at all times – this is one who feeds his children when they are young."[3]

He answered: "But it is written clearly: 'Let him not come at all times into the holy place.'[4] With '*tzedaka* at all times' one still does not merit to enter into the gate of holiness." And for him, the gate of holiness was love of the Jewish people.

When one of his followers turned to him and requested to show him the way to achieve fear of Heaven, he answered: "The proven path to fear of Heaven is love of the Jewish people."

And he would say: "Whenever I feel deep inside myself love of my children, more than I love another Jew, I have not yet reached the attribute of love of the Jewish people."

This was Reb Zusha's prayer every morning after he got out of bed and ritually washed his hands: "Master of the Universe, may it be Your will that You shower blessing and success, life and health, and abundant sustenance on all the Jews, the children of Your mercy."

---

3. Ketubot 50a.
4. Lev. 16:2.

He used to say: "I wish I would merit to love a Jewish tzaddik as the Blessed Holy One loves the worst Jew."

And sometimes he would say: "I love the evil one who knows he is evil, more than a tzaddik who knows he is a tzaddik."

IN THE MERIT OF CHILDREN YOU WILL SAVE THE PARENTS

Reb Elimelekh had difficulty finding any merits or good deeds in himself; he did not even know by what merit he was alive. One unique merit he agreed that he possessed – and he even announced publicly that for the sake of that merit he was permitted to live in the world – was that he took care of the sustenance of his son, Rabbi Elazar, who was dependent on him.

BREAD TO EAT AND CLOTHING TO WEAR

Rabbi Mendel of Rimanov was sitting among many guests around the table of Reb Elimelekh of Lizhensk, but he himself was not eating. Reb Elimelekh asked him, "Mendel, why are you not eating?"

Rabbi Mendel answered, "No one gave me a plate."

Reb Elimelekh said to him:"This is a sign that they forgot you." He ordered someone to bring Mendel some food. They brought him his portion, but still Mendel did not eat.

Again Reb Elimelekh asked him, "Mendel, why are you not eating?"

Rabbi Mendel replied, "This time they forgot to bring me a spoon."

Reb Elimelekh said with a bit of anger: "Mendel, you should be asking not only for a meal, but always ask the Blessed One at the same time for a plate and a spoon too."

Mendel heard what his teacher said and engraved it in his being as if it were a seal upon his heart.

Teshuva

THIS IS THE BLESSING[1]

Reb Zusha was among the favorite students of the Maggid of Mezritch.

There is a story about a man who arrived at the court of the Maggid of Mezritch asking that the tzaddik receive him and give him a blessing. Reb Zusha, who was there at the time, looked at the guest and recognized him as a serious sinner who had no thoughts of *teshuva* (repentance). Reb Zusha was not able to avoid the storm of feelings in his heart toward the man, whose words did not match the feelings in his heart, so he said to him in an angry tone: "Sinner that you are! How are you not ashamed to stand face-to-face with our holy rabbi?"

The guest was taken aback by Reb Zusha's harsh words, and with a bowed head he left the home of the Maggid and disappeared. Reb Zusha followed the man with his eyes as he left the house of the Maggid without saying a word and felt remorse for the insulting words that he had just said to him.

When he told this to his rabbi, the great Maggid said to him: "Every morning we begin our daily prayers with the verse 'How fair are your tents, Yaakov!'[2] so that we will merit seeing only good qualities in the tents of Yaakov. And this is the blessing which I bestow on you this day: May it

1. Deut. 33:1.
2. Num. 24:5.

be God's will that you always see only the positive attributes found in every Jew – even if his sins are as numerous as the seeds in a pomegranate. And our ancient sages already taught us: 'Even though Jews sin, the Blessed Holy One deals with them as sheep' (treats them leniently and forgives their sins)."[3]

Hasidim say that the words of rebuke which the Maggid of Mezritch pronounced at that time to his faithful student penetrated deeply into his heart. And from then on Reb Zusha no longer reprimanded sinners but delivered to every Jew an abundance of love. And when a sinner came to him and shook his hand, a new spirit engulfed him and he immediately had thoughts of repentance.

BOTH OF US WILL REPENT

One summer day, in the heat of the day, Reb Zusha was sitting in the courtyard next to his house to cool off a bit. A man approached him with a request for a written document declaring him free of sin, in order that he might have his *kapota* (long black coat worn by hasidic men) returned to him. Reb Zusha was surprised and did not understand what he was talking about. The man explained that some hasidic men had grabbed him, torn off his *kapota,* told him that he was known to have committed a certain sin, and informed him that they would not return the *kapota* unless he could bring a document from Reb Zusha stating that he was innocent, or that he had repented.

Reb Zusha said to him, "And how will I know if you are really innocent?"

The man pleaded with him: "What does it matter to you? Please give me this document so I can save my coat!" And when he saw that nothing he said could persuade Reb Zusha to give him the document, he became angry and said, "Even if I pleaded with a priest, he would take pity on me!"

When Reb Zusha heard these words, he became very angry and shouted in a loud voice:"Woe is me, that I caused a Jew to speak such words!" He became so agitated that he fell into the sewer-pit in the courtyard. Many neighbors and passersby in the street gathered and lifted

3. Midrash Rabba 24:3.

him from the pit, brought him to his room, removed his clothes, gave him dry clothing, and laid him on his bed to rest. And Reb Zusha lay in his bed and shouted: "Woe is me that I caused a Jew to say bad things!"

And as soon as the panic erupted in the courtyard over Reb Zusha's fall into the pit, that same man ran to a nearby garden and hid between the bushes so he would not be seen. There he began to consider the words of Reb Zusha and had thoughts of repentance. When he saw that the Jews who helped Reb Zusha had left, he came out of hiding, went to Reb Zusha's room, and begged him to help him find a healing for his sins, since he was now repenting.

Reb Zusha said to him: "Woe is me! You are thinking of the *kapota,* not of repentance."

"No, Rabbi!" said the man. I am completely forgoing the *kapota,* as long as you give me a way to repent."

When Reb Zusha saw that the man was truly repenting, he arose from his bed, sat on the ground, and said to the man. "Therefore, let us both repent together."

And they both began to cry a great deal, to the point that the man repented completely from the depth of his heart and became a true God-fearing man for the rest of his life.

THE PLEDGE

Once on Rosh HaShana the tzaddikim Rabbi Levi Yitzḥak of Berdichev, Reb Zusha of Anipoli, Rabbi Mordekhai of Neshkhiz, and the Rebuker of Polnoye were with the Saba of Shpoli. After the meal these five pillars of the world arose from the table and went to a special room to drink mead and discuss matters of redemption and the times before the coming of the Messiah.

During the discussion Reb Zusha said to the Rebuker of Polnoye: "You are more guilty than any of us in this matter that is delaying the coming of the Messiah, since you rebuke people of Israel. So why are you not succeeding with your words of rebuke in causing the people to repent?"

Immediately the Saba of Shpoli jumped to his feet and said, "I understand why Reb Zusha speaks in this way." Raising his hand to heaven, he said: "Master of the Universe, I make a pledge to You, that by reprimands and afflictions Jews will not return to the good. So why do You punish them with no purpose? Surely You foresee, Father in heaven, what will happen at the end. Therefore I ask that act as a good Father to the Jews. As a father who has mercy on his child, even if the child does not walk on the right path, so may You have mercy on us and on all Jews."

The grandfather spoke in a powerful, tearful voice. And all those who were listening cried with him.

RETURN US TO YOU, LORD, AND WE SHALL RETURN[4]

Reb Zusha would say: "What does this verse mean: 'You return man to dust, and You decreed: Repent, children of man!'"[5] He explained: "King David, of blessed memory, would complain, plead, and protest before the Blessed One, saying: Master of the Universe, Father of mercy and forgiveness, 'You return man to dust' if You oppress man with affliction. Can a mortal, despairing and punished, when he is in the situation of 'returning to dust,' consider his ways in order to repent? Surely the thoughts of his heart are mixed up and his sorrow confuses his mind. On the contrary, You who are full of mercy and truth, please grant his needs from Your full and broad hand in order that his mind be clear and at peace as is fitting, and I promise you that they all will return in complete repentance."

THE BOOK IS OPEN

Reb Zusha had a notebook in which he wrote his bad deeds and thoughts. In the evening he would cry so much that the tears dripping from his eyes would erase the letters.

Reb Elimelekh and Reb Zusha had another brother who was the owner of a tavern in a village. The students of Reb Elimelekh decided to travel to this brother and examine his character, since they felt sure that he too was not a simple man.

They came to him and saw that he was standing all day selling liquor to non-Jews. They did not see any good qualities in him, but they did see that he was frequently holding a notebook and writing something in it.

4. Lam. 5:21..

5. Ps. 90:3.

They asked him if he would give them permission to spend the night in his house, and he agreed. At night, when the tavern was closed and the family was asleep, they heard him read from a notebook and burst out crying. They could not restrain themselves and went to him and asked him for an explanation. The man replied in innocence that this was his normal custom: every day when it seemed to him that he had committed a sin or thought about a transgression, he would write this in his notebook, and at night he would not go to sleep until he repented with a full heart. He then added that he knew his repentance had been accepted when he saw that the writing was erased from the notebook; then he knew that his sin was also erased in heaven.

EXAMINING THE SOUL

Once during *Seuda Shlishit,* when Reb Zusha was sitting in the company of his Hasidim, he told the story of what had happened to him and his brother Reb Elimelekh in the years when they were in exile and had wandered penniless from place to place.

On that occasion heavy snow fell all day and night on a road that was deep in mud, making the journey increasingly difficult for the holy brothers. The bitter cold penetrated their bones and added to the afflictions that they had accepted on themselves willingly and with love. For three days not a crumb of food had touched their mouths. It was not because they could not obtain food, but because they had taken on themselves to fast for three days.

In the evening, when they saw before their eyes the familiar chimney rising above the Jewish tavern in one of the towns, they felt some relief in their tired souls, knowing that in a little while they would find rest for their feet. Once inside the tavern the holy brothers recited Minḥa, the afternoon prayer, then studied their regular lessons and recited Maariv, the evening prayer. Afterward they broke their prolonged fast with a slice of salted bread and a glass of water.

When they had eaten, Reb Zusha prepared to recite *Keriat Shema*[6] and get into bed. The two of them were exhausted from the day's hardships, and in a few hours they had to arise to recite *tikkun ḥatzot* in order

6. Prayers centering on the passage from Deuteronomy, recited at bedtime.

to continue from there in their sacred service, in study of Torah and in prayer for the next day.

When Reb Elimelekh noticed that Reb Zusha was preparing to get into bed, he said in a reproachful tone: "Zusha, Zusha! Are you thinking of going to bed without doing an accounting of your soul for this past day?"

Reb Zusha admitted: "Indeed, you are right, my dear brother. We must do the accounting of our souls." The two of them resolved with renewed strength to perform an accounting of the past day.

Only after he had cried his eyes out for a long while, shedding tears of regret and repentance, did Reb Elimelekh permit himself to lie on the earth and catch a short nap on the cold ground.

THE HOLY SOCIETY

Reb Zusha told the following story to Rabbi Shneur Zalman of Liadi, author of the *Tanya:*

My righteous brother Reb Elimelekh once sat in a room next to the room of the Maggid of Mezritch. Suddenly he heard the Maggid calling to him. He entered the Maggid's room, and the Maggid said to him: "Are you listening, Elimelekh, to what they are saying in heaven? 'Love of Jews means to love a complete sinner the same as a complete tzaddik.'" The Maggid added: "The tzaddik has the power to arouse spiritual strength hidden within every soul and to give it strength to repent."

In the morning Reb Elimelekh told these things to his friends.

"Therefore," they said, "we must begin the work." They spoke a great deal among themselves about the meaning of the statements they heard, together with stories and sayings of the ancient sages about *baalei teshuva* (those who repent).

During this conversation a guest entered and listened to their words. Suddenly he broke out in laughter and began to mock this group which was meeting to talk about "fantasies" of Torah and repentance.

Ignoring his taunting, the members of the group stood up to pray with great enthusiasm and with tears, and after the prayers they recited passages from the book of Psalms with fervor and passion. The guest sat and laughed at these idlers and their prayers. And the members of the group began to speak to him and to describe how precious every Jewish soul is in the eyes of the Blessed One. They continued speaking until finally they succeeded in arousing him to repent, and after a few days he became a complete *baal teshuva*.

THE HOLINESS OF TEFILLIN

There was a custom in Berdichev that the *gabbai* of the *ḥevra kadisha* (burial society) would take possession of the tefillin of those who died and would sell them for the benefit of the burial society.

It happened once that the tzaddik Rabbi Levi Yitzḥak of Berdichev came to the *gabbai* and asked him to show him all the pairs of tefillin found in his possession, as he wanted to select a pair of tefillin for himself. The *gabbai* showed him all the pairs of tefillin he had, and the tzaddik chose a pair.

The *gabbai* understood that the tzaddik would not go to the *ḥevra kadisha* just to buy tefillin, and that surely there must be some special reason why he wanted this particular pair. So he said to the tzaddik, "Rabbi, you can buy any pair of tefillin except this one. This pair I will not sell."

The tzaddik pleaded with him to sell him just this pair. Finally the *gabbai* said to him, "I will agree to sell to the rabbi this pair of tefillin, on condition that he tell me what is the nature of this pair, and that he explain to me why he's chasing after them."

The tzaddik replied: "The holy brothers Reb Elimelekh and Reb Zusha were accustomed to wander through towns and villages in order to bring sinners to repentance. Whenever they would come to a certain place to sleep, one of them would turn to the other, as a sinner turns to a rabbi, and would cry and wail about his 'sins' and beg the rabbi to help him repent, and would then detail for him all the sins that the owner of that place had committed, as if he himself had committed them. The owner, hearing these things, would remember that he had committed the same sins and would be aroused to repentance.

"Once they came to a certain village and stayed overnight, as was their custom, in a Jewish house in that village. At night Reb Zusha began to cry and ask his brother to help him repent, saying that all his life he had not inspected his tefillin, and now he had inspected them and seen that they were empty, with none of the required passages, so that it turned out that all his life it had been as if he had never worn tefillin. And Reb Elimelekh began to rebuke him about that, exaggerating the whole matter.

"Their host heard all these words, and suddenly an idea flashed into his mind: I too have never inspected my tefillin! Immediately he ran to get his tefillin, and opened them. They were empty, with none of the required passages! Frightened, the man approached the holy brothers, confessed to them that he had "also" committed the transgression regarding tefillin, and wept and pleaded with them to help him repent.

"Reb Elimelekh said to Reb Zusha: 'Write the passages for this man immediately. And while you write, your intention should be to draw down into the passages such light that it will cover all the time that he did not wear tefillin during his whole life.' Reb Zusha wrote the passages, placed them in the tefillin boxes, and handed them to the man. But the light and the holiness of those tefillin were more than that man could tolerate, and not many days passed before the man died in Berdichev.

"And these," concluded the tzaddik of Berdichev, "are the tefillin that ended up in the possession of the *ḥevra kadisha*."

THE SERVANT WHO REBELLED

It happened once that Reb Elimelekh ordered his servant to take a strap and go with him to the forest to whip a servant who rebelled against his master.

When they reached the forest Reb Elimelekh lay down on the ground and said to his servant: "I am the rebellious servant. Take the strap and count; hit me and do not hesitate. I am a sinner and a transgressor."

BEFORE HIM THERE IS NO FORGETTING

Reb Elimelekh would say: "A person must repent for his sin and for the sin that came before that one, since 'one sin leads to another,'[7] and so on until the first sin of *Adam HaRishon,* and even for him we must always repent.

7. Avot 4:2.

"When I was a nursling, I bit the breasts of my mother, and even for that I repent."

IN THE DARK OF NIGHT

Reb Elimelekh could not go to sleep at night if even one small coin was left in his home. Whenever he had difficulty sleeping, they searched for coins in the pocket of old garments or in discarded boxes. If they found one, he would immediately drop it in a charity box.

It happened once in wintertime that the Hasid Rabbi Leibush of Shidlovitz came to Lizhensk after midnight. There was a heavy snowstorm and thick darkness. Because of his exhaustion from traveling, Rabbi Leibush did not go to Reb Elimelekh to receive a welcome, since it was not proper to come to the rabbi in a bad mood. He went to an inn and went to sleep.

It was the custom that when a Hasid traveled to Reb Elimelekh, his friends would send with him notes and presents. Traveling on the roads was difficult, and not many merited to travel to the rabbi. Rabbi Leibush brought in his satchel notes and presents both from local citizens and from people of other cities through which he passed on his way to Lizhensk.

That night after midnight Reb Elimelekh could not sleep. His family rushed to search for coins in the pockets of his clothing and in the drawers of his desk, even in places where coins are not usually found. They searched but found nothing. Reb Elimelekh said to them, "Perhaps a Hasid came to the inn in the city and brought money, and it is treated as if it were in my bag."

They made rounds of the inns in the city until they found the one where Rabbi Leibush was staying. The rabbi's messengers asked Rabbi Leibush to come immediately to the rabbi for a welcome.

Rabbi Leibush got up from his bed, dressed himself, took all the notes and presents and left. Reb Elimelekh greeted him, spoke with him a bit regarding his trip, asked him about the welfare of their friends in his city, and took from him the notes and presents. Then he sent him back to his inn to sleep, with instructions to send him immediately the wagon driver and the horses that had brought him to Lizhensk, since it was an urgent matter for him. Rabbi Leibush went to the inn to send the wagon driver.

The wagon driver was a simple man, a boor and ignoramus. In his whole life he had never seen a tzaddik, and he had no idea what a tzaddik was. After he had filled his stomach with food and added to it some drink, he had lain down behind the warm stove and sunk into a deep, sweet sleep. Rabbi Leibush awakened him and asked him to go right away to Reb Elimelekh.

The wagon driver became angry and shouted insults and curses. "What do I have to do with your rabbi, to go to him in the dark of night and in a snowstorm?" he snarled. "How dare you wake me from my sleep, a Hasid like you? If your rabbi needs me, let him disturb himself to come to me!" Rabbi Leibush pleaded with the wagon driver to go immediately, since the matter was extremely urgent. The wagon driver increased his insults and curses and turned his face to the wall, yelling: "I will not go at night to your rabbi. Get out of here, foolish Hasid. I am sleeping, I am sleeping!"

But the wagon driver did not fall asleep. He was surprised and puzzled: Why was he not sleeping? Usually he fell asleep right away, sometimes almost before he could get undressed. He tossed and turned and still could not sleep. Maybe the rabbi was causing it, forcing him to get up and go to him in the dark of night? The wagon driver was angry at the rabbi and at the foolish Hasid who brought this trouble on him. He even spoke words of anger and taunting in a loud voice.

When Rabbi Leibush the Hasid heard the angry taunts of the wagon driver, and saw that he was not sleeping, again he tried to persuade him to go. But the wagon driver held his own with insults and curses.

Suddenly the wagon driver changed his mind and started to excuse himself, saying that he could not go because he was tired. He wanted to go but could not, as he had pains in his body and it was chilly outside.

Rabbi Leibush said to him, "You can if you only want to."

"How can I go when I do not know the way to the house of your rabbi?" said the wagon driver.

Rabbi Leibush answered him: "If you really want to, you can find the way to the home of Reb Elimelekh. Keep going until you see light in the window of the house. In all the other houses it is dark, but in the rabbi's house a candle is burning. You will get to the rabbi; you will find him." The wagon driver got up and dressed, but he did not cease spewing insults and curses till he stood at the door of the rabbi's home.

Reb Elimelekh rebuked him: "Evil one, admit all your sins of robbery and burglary."

At first the wagon driver spoke loudly to the rabbi and protested that he was innocent of any sin. Reb Elimelekh stared at him with a probing and penetrating look. The wagon driver's face quivered and he broke out in a cry of confession: "Rabbi, woe is me! I am evil!"

The wagon driver told Reb Elimelekh the details of his sins and cried with a broken heart: "Rabbi, Rabbi, what will happen to me? Maybe, Heaven forbid, I am a condemned soul and beyond repair."

Reb Elimelekh comforted him, saying, "The Blessed One says, 'No one is banished before Me.' One who wants to become pure will be helped. And I promise you that if you repent your sins will be atoned for."

The blessing was fulfilled. The wagon driver became a complete *baal teshuva,* even an outstanding student of Torah and a devout person.

A BROKEN HEART

Once on Rosh Ḥodesh Elul Reb Elimelekh sat with his head lowered, full of sorrow and distress, and said: "The Days of Judgment are getting closer, and how can I lift my head to Heaven? Are not my sins too many to count?"

Thus he sat for a long while. Finally he got up and said, "Good. I will stand with a broken heart before my Creator on the Day of Judgment."

THE BEST HEALER

Reb Elimelekh once stayed with his teacher, Rabbi Shmelke of Nikolsburg. In the beit midrash he saw his master standing on the pulpit and preaching before the congregation about a deep passage which was not understood by most of the listeners. When Rabbi Shmelke concluded his sermon, Reb Elimelekh went up to the pulpit and told this story:

"A king received as a present a horse of incomparable beauty. The king loved the horse deeply without measure. After a while the horse became ill, and there was no doctor in the country who knew how to heal it. The king saw that his horse was dying and no one could save it. He was very sad. He sent an announcement to all the citizens of the country, seeking someone who could heal the sick horse.

"A farmer came and said, 'My lord the king, do not trust physicians. Let me take the horse, and I will bring it complete healing.'

"The king said: 'Farmer, did you come to mock me? The leading doctors in my country are without guidance, and you will find a cure for the horse, which is mortally ill? Or perhaps you acquired special knowledge in the science of healing from the medical scholars? Maybe instead of hastening a cure for my beloved horse, you are liable to hasten its death, Heaven forbid. Therefore, you should know, farmer, woe to you if you do not succeed in healing my horse.'

"The farmer replied, 'My lord the king, I did not come because I have more knowledge than the medical scholars, to heal your horse. I am not an arrogant fool to attribute to myself superior wisdom in medical science. But I am not like your scholarly doctors. Their skill is to heal kings, but my skill is to heal horses.'"

Reb Elimelekh concluded: "My master and my teacher, the light of the exile, Rabbi Shmelke, possesses strength in expressing beautiful, inspiring phrases and deep, wise sayings that serve as healing balms to intelligent people and to great scholars, but not to the masses. By contrast, Elimelekh is ignorant of Torah and lacking in deep wisdom. Therefore he will tell them simple words, which are understood even by those who have no brain. Elimelekh tells you that you are rebellious children, servants who are dominated by your evil inclination, who persist in your stubbornness. Children of Avraham, Yitzḥak, and Yaakov, repent!"

When the congregation heard the stinging words of Reb Elimelekh, they all burst into tears.

GOD CREATED FOR ME A NEW HEART

Rabbi David of Lelov sat for six years studying Torah and praying and afflicting himself with fasts and self-mortification. After that he sat another six consecutive years fasting from Shabbat to Shabbat. And yet his heart misgave him, for he feared that he had not yet reached spiritual perfection.

At that time Reb Elimelekh became famous as a tzaddik and healer of souls, so Rabbi David traveled to Lizhensk to see him.

On the eve of the holy Shabbat he entered the home of Reb Elimelekh amid the rest of the guests to receive a welcome. When Reb Elimelekh looked at his face he refused to greet him and even turned his face away from him toward the wall. Rabbi David left the house with a broken heart and returned to his inn. He walked here and there, deep in thought. He was perplexed: What was his sin and what was his failure, that Reb Elimelekh rejected him in shame?

The owner of the inn saw that he was enveloped in sorrow. He said to him: "Young man, 'worry weighs down the heart.'"[8] Rabbi David told him what had happened.

The innkeeper comforted him: "Maybe it was an accident, or a mistake." He advised him to go to the beit midrash and stand and pray in the corner, and after the prayers, before Kiddush, approach Reb Elimelekh and extend his hand to him with "*shalom aleikhem*," and perhaps he would merit to receive the rabbi's greeting.

Rabbi David did so. He stood in the corner to pray. But because of the depth of his fervor, he began to move here and there all over the beit midrash, praying in a loud voice. After the prayer he approached Reb Elimelekh to extend his hand in greeting. Reb Elimelekh rebuffed him. "What has this frightened man to do with me?" he said. "I do not like frightened people."

Rabbi David returned to the inn with a broken heart and cried bitterly for a long time. He didn't sleep all night. He decided in his mind not to be seen by Reb Elimelekh again but to leave Lizhensk at the end of Shabbat. But for the third Shabbat meal he could not restrain himself, and entered the beit midrash of Reb Elimelekh while they were setting the table.

Reb Elimelekh was teaching Torah with enormous enthusiasm. Suddenly he said: "There are young men who come to me from faraway places, who occupy themselves with Torah and divine service and with

8. Prov. 12:25.

harrowing self-mortification for many years. And after all this effort they see themselves fit for the Divine Presence to envelop them, and they come to me so that I can relieve their small defects and extend to them the holy spirit. But they are deceiving themselves. They have not yet even begun to serve the Creator or to be truly God-fearing. And since they are misled into believing that they have already come far with Torah and divine service, they have become very proud. This is a sign to them that they are full of ulterior motives – and every ulterior motive has a bad smell."

When Rabbi David heard this, he had a change of heart, and a great fear overcame him: perhaps, Heaven forbid, he had descended to the lowest level of loathsomeness, and there was no cure for his soul! He sat alone in the corner of the dark beit midrash and broke out in heavy sobs, which no one heard because of the singing that resounded in the beit midrash. At that moment he decided that after Havdala he would enter the room of Reb Elimelekh and lay his plea before him and not be put off anymore until he was shown the path to repentance.

After Havdala he approached the door to Reb Elimelekh's room and opened it very slowly. When Reb Elimelekh saw him. he got up from his chair and went toward him. He greeted him with a smiling face, saying, "Blessed is your coming, Rabbi David, joy of my heart." He gave him a big hug and spoke to him with great love.

Rabbi David asked, "Rabbi, am I not the man that you expelled twice?"

Reb Elimelekh answered, "You are not that man. You are a completely different person. You are David, the light of my eyes."

YOU NEED A TEACHER

It happened that Rabbi Yaakov Yitzḥak, later known as the Seer of Lublin, was traveling to see his teacher, Reb Elimelekh, and entered the beit midrash of a small town on the way. There he heard the local rabbi reciting the prayers with great enthusiasm. He assumed that the rabbi was a follower of Hasidism, and at the first opportunity asked him which tzaddik he had served. The rabbi responded that he had never served a tzaddik but had read many hasidic books.

Rabbi Yaakov Yitzḥak was puzzled, for he had understood that the hasidic way cannot be learned from books alone but only from sitting at the feet of a master. He asked the rabbi to accompany him to see Reb Elimelekh, and they set forth together.

When they arrived at Reb Elimelekh's court, the tzaddik did not greet them as usual, but turned his face away; there was nothing for them to do but go back to the inn. Later Rabbi Yaakov Yitzḥak returned alone. Reb Elimelekh greeted him as usual but immediately reproached him for bringing him a man in whom the divine image was defaced.

Rabbi Yaakov Yitzḥak explained how he had met with the rabbi. Reb Elimelekh then said, "When a man attempts to learn these things by himself, his service is likely to be tainted with pride and ulterior motives. Then he may think that he feels a fiery devotion, but the fire in fact comes from the *klipat noga,* the sphere governed by the planet Venus, where good and evil are mixed. And by himself he will never know the difference."

Rabbi Yaakov Yitzḥak went back to the inn where he had left the rabbi and told him what Reb Elimelekh had said. Brokenhearted, the rabbi went back to Reb Elimelekh's house and entered his door with fear and trembling. This time Reb Elimelekh accepted him as his student, and with the tzaddik's help he was able to do *teshuva* and become a true Hasid.

AS LONG AS THE CANDLE IS BURNING

In the neighborhood of Reb Elimelekh lived a furrier, whose name was also Elimelekh. He was accustomed to work until late at night.

Once after midnight the furrier was tired from his long day's work and fell asleep. Reb Elimelekh heard through the thin wall the wife of the furrier waking her husband and yelling at him: "Elimelekh, Elimelekh, repair the fur as long as the candle is still burning!"

"These words," said Reb Elimelekh, "have run in my ears constantly from that night on, and give me no rest."

The human soul is compared to a candle: "A man's soul is the lamp (candle) of G-d."[9] From the simple furrier Reb Elimelekh took the

9. Ibid. 20:27.

message never to give up. As long as the candle is burning you can still make repairs. As long as there's life, there's still time to make spiritual repairs as well. We can still do *teshuva* – make positive changes in our lives – and set right all the things that are wrong.

PROPER TESHUVA

"Return, rebellious children" (Jeremiah 3:14).
Do *teshuva* on your repentance.
Is this the way to return in repentance?

– Reb Zusha of Anipoli

This World and the Next

THE *ḤAZZAN* OF THE BESHT

It happened once on the day before Shabbat that a *ḥazzan,* a bass singer, and another musician came to the beit midrash of Reb Elimelekh. The *ḥazzan* asked Reb Elimelekh to permit him to lead the prayers for *Kabbalat Shabbat* (welcoming the Shabbat). Reb Elimelekh was apprehensive, lest the *ḥazzan* confuse him in his prayers. However, his son, Rabbi Elazar, persuaded him to permit the *ḥazzan* to lead the prayers, in order not to embarrass him, and also because he was the *ḥazzan* in the beit midrash of the Besht; everyone called him "the *ḥazzan* of the Besht."

When the *ḥazzan* began to pray, Reb Elimelekh's soul was moved from the power of the sweetness in his voice, and a deep illumination entered his soul. He truly felt the radiance of the pleasantness and majesty of God.

All his life Reb Elimelekh was despicable and loathsome in his own eyes. He suffered from crippling fears that he was a totally evil person, just a proud beggar, a nothing. But when the *hazzan* sang the beautiful hymn *"Hashem malakh ge'ut lavesh"* (The Lord reigns, robed in majesty),[1] it seemed to Reb Elimelekh that the gates of melody opened before him and he entered the great heavenly sanctuary, where he sat before the Blessed Holy One, while the ministering angels took

1. Ps. 93:1.

delight in him and said to him, "Happy are you, Elimelekh, for you are a tzaddik."

Out of great concern that he become arrogant, he began to shout in the middle of the prayer that they should remove the *ḥazzan* from the pulpit. But suddenly a terrible dread seized him.

After the prayers Reb Elimelekh approached the *hazzan,* wished him "Shabbat Shalom," and asked his forgiveness, saying that he did not do that, Heaven forbid, to embarrass him, but out of fear that he would lose consciousness because of the extreme sweetness of his prayers.

After Shabbat Reb Elimelekh asked the *ḥazzan* to tell him about the holiness of the Besht and to recount the story of how he became a *ḥazzan*. The *ḥazzan* answered the second question first, and the first question last. He said that he became a *ḥazzan* at the order of the Besht, of blessed memory, and this is his account of how it happened:

"Once I asked the Besht: 'What should be my occupation?' The Besht said to me: 'You should be a *ḥazzan*.' I said, 'I am not a musician.' The Besht said to me: 'I will connect you with the world of music and you will become a musician.' The Besht, of blessed memory, also said to me: 'You should know that you will be on the pulpit and lead the prayers for the last time on the day they chase you from the pulpit.' I understood from his holy words that after they chase me from the pulpit, I will die."

Reb Elimelekh said to him: "Will you please tell me a story about the Besht, of blessed memory?"

The *ḥazzan* said: "Once the Besht was smiling for no apparent reason, and his students asked him why. The Besht told them this true story. In a faraway country a dignitary built a very beautiful palace, which took him several years to complete. At that time a certain tzaddik went to the synagogue to recite the afternoon prayers. Suddenly a very heavy rain began to fall. This tzaddik went into the palace and found shelter from the heavy rain. When the tzaddik left the palace after the rain had stopped, the palace collapsed. 'How shall I not laugh,' said the Besht, 'about the ways in which this world works? This palace came into existence only to serve as a shelter for a great tzaddik for a short time. Once the sparks were assembled, what purpose was there for the building?'"

When Reb Elimelekh heard this story, he understood that the *ḥazzan* was created by the Besht, who connected him to the world of music only for one prayer in his beit midrash to save him from the fear of pride. When the prayer was completed the *ḥazzan* had no more shelter and was flying in space like a naked body, a lump of loathsome pride.

The next day the *ḥazzan* fell sick, and by evening he died. On Wednesday of the same week, the bass singer came to the congregational office and said: "Please call the *ḥevra kadisha* to dig a grave for me. The *ḥazzan* came to me last night in a dream and said that in *Gan Eden* they were giving him the honor of welcoming Shabbat in honor of the Besht and repeating for him the melody of *'Hashem malakh ge'ut lavesh.'* But the *ḥazzan* does not want to lead prayers for the congregation in *Gan Eden* without a bass voice."

From this Reb Elimelekh understood that he too was wanted in heaven to hear *"Lekhu Neranena"*[2] on this Shabbat in *Gan Eden*. He lay down on his bed and closed his eyes, and his soul departed with the sweetness of the melody of *"Hashem malakh ge'ut lavesh."*

THE BOOKBINDER

Once Reb Elimelekh fell ill. His illness worsened and he died. His soul lingered in heaven for several days and nights, while his students stood by his body and asked for heavenly mercy. Eventually, his soul was returned to his body, he awakened from his long sleep, and when he recovered, he related what he had seen and heard in the Upper World.

When he ascended to heaven, the great rabbi, Rabbi Avraham Azoulai, author of *Ḥesed L'Avraham*, came to see him and went with him on walks in the fresh breeze of the day. As they walked he asked him: "What is the new path which you and your holy brother Reb Zusha are promoting? This is an important subject, and I must study it. I have been privileged to write ten books, all of which are accepted in the Upper World, where the tzaddikim sit and study them in *Gan Eden*, but never have they made an impression in heaven. Yet regarding your

2. "Come let us sing joyfully to Hashem" (Ps. 96:1), the opening words of the *Kabbalat Shabbat* service.

holy brother, who never wrote a single book, the heavens and heavens of heavens are in awe of his words. When he sits and lingers an hour before prayer, as did the early Hasidim, and has not reached even the entrance to the temple of prayer, there is already a commotion in the Upper World, and they are all in awe and trembling; how much more so when he stands during the actual prayer. And another thing: come and I will show you a beautiful sanctuary where a great person from among your group dwells, whose path is your path."

They came to an orchard with beautiful fruit trees, whose smell was like the aroma of the garden which God blessed. They strolled in paths between flower beds and listened to the conversation of holy angels coming from between the trees. They walked a long time until they reached a hill. They climbed up and up, and when they reached the top they saw in the distance a towering, exalted sanctuary.

Rabbi Azoulai said: "Look at the magnificent building! It is a sanctuary of marble where your friend Rabbi Shmelke of Nikolsburg dwells and spreads Torah to his students. Some weeks ago he came to us and established a yeshiva, and since then he orders the souls who arrive from the netherworld to come to his yeshiva. Tell me please, Elimelekh, what is the innovation you are making in your beit midrash? It seems to be something important." Reb Elimelekh answered him, and Rabbi Azoulai thought about it and accepted the answer. Then he left and went on his way.

Having heard about the yeshiva of the tzaddik Rabbi Shmelke in heaven, he decided to go there, to befriend him and to take in the fragrance of his Torah. He went there and found a certain man standing outside near the entrance to the house. He approached him and saw that he was a simple Jew from Lizhensk, whose name was Mordechai the bookbinder. He was quite surprised: Where did this man come from? Is he not still living? He looked at him carefully and understood from the fact that he was garbed in a tallit and white linen shrouds that he was among the deceased. He asked him: "Mordechai the bookbinder, what are you doing here, and how did you merit being near this yeshiva?" "Holy Rabbi," Mordechai said, "had they heard in heaven that you call me Mordechai, and not Reb Mordechai, they would reprimand you. This is how the heavenly court called me."

Hearing this, Reb Elimelekh was even more surprised. "Reb Mordechai," he asked, "what is your interest in this yeshiva? Are you not a simple Jew? So who brought you here?" He answered: "It is true, I am a simple Jew, just as the rabbi says, and normally I have no place here. But there is more to this. And since you asked me, I will tell you everything that happened to me from the day I came to heaven, and you will understand why I am here.

"This is the story. After my death I was brought before the heavenly court, and they began to judge me and check my past deeds. I stood there trembling, not knowing what was going to happen to me. I saw the ministering angels bringing my good and bad deeds and placing them on the scale. At times the good deeds prevailed, and at times my bad deeds, until at the end the faults outweighed the merits and they decided to send me to *Gehinom*. I accepted the judgment, I left the court, and in sorrow and shame I went to the place assigned me. The road is long, and the farther I went from the place where I was, the hotter it grew, and my pain grew without measure.

"But when I came close to the area of *Gehinom*, which was burning with fire, two officers of the court grabbed me in haste and brought me back to the heavenly court. I saw wagons full of sacks passing by, and it seemed to me that these sacks were mine. Amazed, I asked myself: Who brought these worn-out sacks to this world, and why were they brought here? I thought a lot about this matter, trying in vain to find the answer. I walked on, and the wagons full of sacks followed me on the road, until I reached the courthouse. When I entered the courthouse I found the members of the court sitting in their places as before, and in front of them were the scales on which they weighed my deeds, and the two pans were balanced just as I had seen them last. The officers who had brought me set me before the judges and then left, and immediately the ministering angels dealt with the wagons standing outside, pushing and carrying the sacks and placing them on the side of merits. As I stood there, the pan of misdeeds which before had prevailed and sunk low began to rise. And as they brought more sacks, the pan of merits went down, and the other one rose upward. Little by little the pan of transgressions rose until the two pans were equal, with the pan of merits almost prevailing.

And this is what happened next: they brought another full sack and placed it on the pan, and this tipped the scale to the side of merit. The judges saw this and many other sacks that had not yet been weighed, so they excused me from the judgment of *Gehinom* and ordered that I be taken to to *Gan Eden*.

"After this decision was made, a heavenly voice announced that from now on my name would no longer be Mordechai, but Reb Mordechai. All that time I stood there in fear, not knowing what was happening: Why did they judge me at first for my misdeeds, and now for my merits? And why did they give me such honor, adding the title 'Reb' before my name? I asked the angels near me but they were silent. I went to the more important angels, and they too did not have an answer. But I did not keep quiet, I did not rest; I went and inquired further, till I found out the following:

"When I left the heavenly court after the first decision, an angel whose name was Guardian of Pages came and stood before the judges, saying that he knew of some merits and had come to defend me.

"They said to him: 'We don't discuss issues once they are finished.'

"He said to them: 'This is said of other judgments, but not of capital crimes, since we learned: "Once the verdict is reached, they bring him out to stone him, as it says, 'Bring out the one who has cursed.'[3] The stoning area was outside the courthouse. One would stand before the entrance to the courthouse, his shawl in his hand; and another would ride on a horse before them at a distance, in order to be seen. If someone says, 'I have an argument for acquittal,' then he would wave the shawl, and the one on horseback would run back to stop the procession. And even if the accused said, 'I have an argument for my own acquittal,' then he would be brought back; and this might happen even four or five times, so long as there was substance to his words. If he was acquitted, he was dismissed; and if not, he was brought out to be stoned. And an announcer would go before him and proclaim, 'So-and-so son of so-and-so is being brought out to be stoned for having committed such and such transgression, and so-and-so and so-and-so are his witnesses.

3. Lev. 24:14.

Anyone who has any knowledge as to his innocence should come and argue for him.'"[4]

"They said to him: 'Say something and explain yourself.'

"He began to speak: 'My masters and my teachers, I have knowledge of the innocence of a Jewish man, and I believe that there is substance to my words. The deceased was a simple man, like the majority of Jews. He did not study Torah, and maybe he was a total ignoramus, and occasionally committed terrible transgressions due to his ignorance; but he is an honest Jew, and the Torah was precious to him, and there was no one in his generation who honored the Torah like him. All his life he bound books accurately and labored with great love in the things that the Blessed Creator desired. And though all the effort that he expended was for his welfare and his pleasure, his work was sacred labor. Much love, fine taste, and beauty he devoted to his skill, and in his whole life nothing emerged from his hand that was not of fine quality. The books which he bound were so dear to him that he did not disparage even empty pages that had not even one letter, pages that served only to preserve the book. How much more so was he careful with lines and letters, not to damage them when he cut the sheets of pages. Furthermore, he treated the sections of sheets that were cut from the holy books as *tashmishei kedusha* (ritual articles), and he placed them in a *geniza* as Jewish law requires. He did not throw them in the trash but gathered them together, placed them in sacks, and brought them to the attic of his house. And if you do not believe me, they rest there now, and with your permission I will go and bring them to you.'

"At that moment a pronouncement was heard in heaven: 'Whoever honors the Torah is honored by humankind and blessed in this world and in the next world.' And the judges saw fit to reconsider their decision. They ordered the officers of the court to bring the sacks from the attic and to bring me to the heavenly court. They brought me back, and the angel brought the sacks, with the permission of the court. On the way back I saw those sacks on the wagons; they were the ones that tipped the scale for me to the side of merit and gave me my place in the World to Come.

4. Mishna Sanhedrin 6:1.

"When I heard this good news, I rejoiced greatly. Here I had been on the threshold of *Gehinom*, and I was saved from its torture by a miracle. But my joy was not complete; other concerns arose that I had not thought of at all until now. I thought that I would go to my final rest and would dwell in peace and harmony with Hashem. But it did not turn out the way I thought.

"Whoever enters *Gan Eden* because he honored the Torah, enters the sanctuary of the Torah; and he must be a student of Torah, so that he will not be like a deaf person among the wise. But as for me – true, I bound books my whole life. I did my work with great love; I folded the sheets with care and arranged them as required. No book ever left my hands with pages mixed up or upside down, I was careful with all the letters, but I did not know what was written in them. From the time I was young I had dealt with books; I knew their titles and chapters, and even the names of the authors, but I had never reached the level of reading them. And now I would have to sit with the great minds of the world, whose books I had bound, yet I didn't understand their simplest discussions.

"Since they saw that this situation was not good for them or for me, they decided to teach me Torah before I came to eternal rest in the sanctuary of the Torah. So I wander, until I merit to reach my final resting place forever. Meanwhile I have gone from yeshiva to yeshiva and have progressed in my studies. I began slowly, with easy material, and later with more difficult material, and all that I heard from my teachers I have kept in my heart. And as far as my mind could absorb, I have persisted with my studies. And my soul understands and grasps the revealed Torah. And now that I have had success in my labors, they told me that I am ready to study the hidden Torah, and they sent me to the yeshiva of the holy Rabbi Shmelke, so I am standing here waiting until they open the gates."

While he was still speaking, the gates opened, and a voice was heard from the house announcing: "Reb Mordechai the bookbinder! A place for you is ready inside and you are standing outside. 'This is the gate to the Lord; tzaddikim shall enter through it.'"[5]

---

5. Ps. 118:19.

Immediately Reb Mordechai left Reb Elimelekh and went inside the house, and the door closed behind him.

At the same time the tzaddik Reb Elimelekh approached the gate and wanted to open it, but it was shut tight. He began to scream, but there was no reply, and as he screamed he awoke and saw himself in the lower world, his body lying in a sea of sweat. Later the sweat passed and the fever left him, but he lay in bed weak and exhausted for days and weeks. God pitied him and sent him a complete healing.

ON THE WEDDING DAY

This story is found in the book *Ohel Elimelekh*. It was originally told by the holy Rabbi Yitzḥak Eizik of Komarno.

In his youth Reb Elimelekh had a good friend, a soul mate, a young man exceptional in Torah study as well as in good deeds. Suddenly the young man fell ill and was close to death. Before he died he asked his friend Reb Elimelekh to raise his son, who would be an orphan, and to be like a father to him.

Reb Elimelekh asked his friend to promise to come to him from heaven and tell him how they judged him in the heavenly court. The young man promised and they shook hands.

Reb Elimelekh fulfilled his promise and took the orphan child into his house to raise him. He taught him Torah and gave him everything he needed. When the child grew to marriageable age, he sought and found for him a lovely and graceful bride, the daughter of fine parents, with a dowry as well. Reb Elimelekh asked the father of the bride if he could host the wedding in his own house in memory of the father of the groom, who had been a frequent guest of his and had studied together with him there. The father of the bride agreed, and so it was. Many people of the city attended, as well as followers of Reb Elimelekh from other cities.

On the day of the wedding the rabbi retired to his special room and did not emerge for a long time. The anticipation and excitement grew among the congregation. The in-laws on the bride's side and the guests on the groom's side were fearful and perplexed, but no one dared to knock on the door of the room lest, Heaven forbid, they interrupt the rabbi in his holy thoughts. Late in the evening, after the congregation had already finished the evening prayers, Reb Elimelekh appeared from his room and went to officiate at the wedding.

After the meal following the marriage ceremony, Reb Elimelekh related to those gathered the reason for the delay in the ceremony. First he spoke about his dear friend, the father of the groom, honoring his memory as he would for a brother. He described the great affection between them; he mentioned the late father's request that he raise his orphan son, and the agreement they had. "I kept my promise," said Reb Elimelekh, "but the father of the groom did not keep his. So I did not want to begin the ceremony until he came and fulfilled his promise. The matter caused me great anxiety."

Reb Elimelekh paused for a short while, immersed in thought. His face, which had shone with the joy of the *simḥa,* was now covered in sadness. The grief which had been hidden in his heart for many years returned and seized him. But although he was subject to sadness, he immediately rallied and called out: "Elimelekh, Elimelekh, even in a time of joy, at the celebration of a bride and groom, you are ready to be captured by the evil inclination of sadness! Elimelekh, run away from this sadness."

He waved his hand in front of his face to chase away the sadness and continued his story: "Elimelekh is stubborn. In his obstinacy he would not proceed to the *ḥuppa* until the father of the groom appeared to him. I looked and saw him standing before me just as he did when he was alive. I said to him: 'Father of the groom, tell me now, how did your judgment go before the heavenly court?' The father of the groom told me this story:

"'When I died I felt no pain or sorrow, and it was as if I were sleeping. When they performed *tahara* (ritual purification) I wanted to chase them away. I did not have the strength to get up. I thought I was dreaming. They closed the grave and no other living person was in the cemetery. I arose from my grave and I seemed to be alive. I asked in surprise: What am I doing in the cemetery? I wanted to go home. I did not know where the gate of the cemetery was. I climbed on the fence and jumped to the other side. I walked on the path to my house. The sun set and it became dark. Then I saw a river and I wanted to cross to the other side, but the water flowed very strongly and I was afraid. I found there two logs, and I wanted to throw them into the river, but I couldn't because the water was too deep. To my great sorrow it began to rain very heavily; my shrouds became wet and there was no road to cross. There was no choice left for me except to return to the cemetery. My desire to return to life and to see the faces of my family was great. I cried and pleaded to the Master of the Universe: "Answer me, just as You answered Jonah from the mighty waves!"

"'Suddenly a man as tall as a giant appeared to me and asked me: "Why are you crying?" I told him: "I miss my family and I cannot go to them." The giant said to me: "Fool that you are, you think that you are alive, and behold, you are dust." He took me, picked me up, and brought me before the heavenly tribunal. They were studying my judgment and did not find any transgressions that would cause them to assign me to *Gehinom*. But since they found some type of mistake, they would not let me enter *Gan Eden* immediately. They decided to bring me to a certain sanctuary that has an entrance to *Gan Eden* and an entrance to *Gehinom*. I was to see the terrible punishments in *Gehinom*, and this would nullify the mistake so that I would be able to enter *Gan Eden*.

"'Immediately they transferred me to the individual in charge to place me in that sanctuary. And when I looked at *Gehinom* I saw many people whom I knew, and I heard the shouts of the tortured. It pained me greatly, and I wished I were blind so that I would not see those terrible scenes, and deaf so that I would not hear the cries of those judged. But when I looked at the faces of the tzaddikim dwelling in *Gan Eden* and enjoying the luster of the Divine Presence, I was not happy, and even felt terrible pain because I was not yet fit for the joys of *Gan Eden*.

"'Since it was almost time for the holy Shabbat, when all the souls are released from *Gehinom*, I asked the person in charge to release me also from my sanctuary. He answered that he did not have permission to do that. I pleaded with him to go to the heavenly court and ask permission. He went and returned and told me that they had given him permission. I went out of the sanctuary. I looked up and saw souls without number flying in the high heavens. I asked: Where are they flying to? They told me: to greet the Shabbat queen. A pure white angel came near. All the souls ran to welcome him; they hugged him and kissed him. I asked:

"Who is this angel?" They told me that this angel was created from the words of the holy Torah which were uttered by Reb Elimelekh.

"'When I heard that I remembered that Reb Elimelekh was my dearest friend from my youth. I greatly rejoiced that he was so important in heaven. I said: "Therefore I also deserve a portion in *Gan Eden*."

"'After Shabbat the person in charge came to take me back to my sanctuary. I told him that I did not want to go there. He said to me: "Why do you refuse? I am just an officer of the court and do as I am told." I told him: "Go to the heavenly court and tell them that I am a friend of Reb Elimelekh, and therefore I do not want to return to my sanctuary." He told them, and they said to him that they agreed with me. But since I had made an agreement with Reb Elimelekh to inform him about what had happened with my judgment, I was required to fulfill my promise. As a reward for this I would not be required to dwell again in the sanctuary between *Gehinom* and *Gan Eden*.

"'So now I came to you to inform you of my judgment. But if I am not mistaken, many years have passed meanwhile.'

"'Yes,' I answered the father of the groom, 'almost eighteen years have passed. When you died your son was one year old, and now he is already getting married.' The father of the groom said to me: 'Hurry and get me out of here and give me a document of release from the world which I can show to the heavenly court as proof that I kept my promise.' I gave him a document of release and I asked him to have the honor of sitting with me until the end of his son's marriage ceremony. He said to me: 'Do not restrain me here even one minute, because you cannot imagine the great joy which a soul has in the next world, and how this world is not important to the soul at all.' I said to him, 'Nevertheless, perhaps you will linger with us here another few minutes, since you came under my protection at the time of the wedding of your son.' He answered me: 'No, no, no,' and left."

And Reb Elimelekh concluded: "Elimelekh learned from this story an important lesson: If this young man, who was a total tzaddik, wandered so many years without finding rest, then how much more shall Elimelekh, who is evil, wander for days and years and be subjected to great suffering."

THE CHANGES IN HIS LIFE

The tzaddik Rabbi David of Lelov once visited Reb Elimelekh. Since he did not have any money to hire a carriage, he went by foot.

On his way he met a Hasid well known in Warsaw as a wealthy man, who was riding in a carriage. Rabbi David asked him where he was going. He replied that he was traveling to Lizhensk to see the tzaddik Reb Elimelekh. Rabbi David asked if he could ride with him in the carriage, and the wealthy man agreed.

The wealthy man thought that Rabbi David was some poor vagabond, and during the journey he mocked him, but Rabbi David restrained himself and did not reply. This is how it was during the entire trip – the wealthy man mocked him, and Rabbi David was silent.

When they reached Lizhensk the wealthy man went in immediately to see the tzaddik. Rabbi David thought it necessary to prepare himself spiritually before going inside, so he waited a while and then entered. Reb Elimelekh spoke with Rabbi David for about two hours. The wealthy man saw that the tzaddik was talking with Rabbi David for a long time, and he understood immediately that he was not a simple man, and he deeply regretted that he had mocked him during the trip.

After he left the tzaddik, Rabbi David turned to the wealthy man and said to him: "Go your way, because I need to stay here for a while." Then he said: "On your way back to your city, when you hear a shout, follow it and you will know what you must do." The wealthy man took heed of Rabbi David's words, and kept them in his heart.

As the wealthy man reached the midpoint of his journey to the city, he suddenly heard someone shouting in Polish. He remembered the words of Rabbi David and rushed to follow the sound, turning off the highway and into the thick of the forest, until he came to a place full of sludge, where he saw someone sinking with his carriage and horses in the mud. He immediately took a thick rope and tied one end to his coach, which stood at a distance in a dry spot, and the other end to the carriage stuck in the mud. Then he seated himself in his coach and whipped his horses, and within a few minutes the horses pulled out the carriage and it passenger.

The man had been in the mud for a long time, and when the wealthy man pulled him out he was filthy and very cold. The wealthy man gave him a warm coat and food and drink till he was comfortable.

"Where are you from?" he asked the man.

"From Warsaw," the man answered.

"I too am from Warsaw," said the wealthy man, "and I am traveling there now, so you can ride together with me and you will be able to rest in my home until you are completely well."

And so it was. When they arrived at the wealthy man's home, he removed his guest's clothing, which was wet and full of mud, gave him a bed, and offered him tea and coffee and all kinds of good food, until he fell asleep. In the morning he was well again and departed with joy and appreciation.

A few days later the man called the wealthy man and asked him: "How can I repay you for all your kindness toward me? If you had not saved me, I would have drowned in the mud or died from exhaustion."

The wealthy man replied that he owed him nothing. "It is enough for me," he said, "that I saved someone from death, and this is my reward and my payment."

The man said to him, "I am an official in this region, so at least tell me your name and address so I will always remember who it was who saved me." He gave him his name and address, and the official wrote it in his memorandum book.

Many years passed. The wheel of fortune turned, and the wealthy man lost all his money. He was compelled to give his business to others; he was even forced to sell his house, his expensive clothing, his furniture, and everything else he owned to keep himself alive. When he had finished selling everything he became a poor, simple beggar. He wandered from city to city and from village to village, and in this terrible condition ten years passed until he had completely forgotten that he was once a wealthy man. After long wandering he reached the city of Warsaw, his former home, and even here he was not embarrassed to hold out his hand and ask for charity from people walking up and down the street.

One day he saw an elegant gentleman traveling in a respectable carriage. He approached the carriage, as was his custom, removed his hat, bowed his head, and stretched out his hand to receive some charity. The gentleman – an official of the region of Warsaw – looked at his face and said to him, "Come closer to me, Jew." The man was frightened and started to run away. The gentleman ordered his servant to apprehend him and bring him back, and the servant did so. The gentleman said to the beggar: "Do not be afraid; I won't do anything to you. I only ask you to tell me your name." The man told him his name.

"Do you recognize me?" asked the official.

"No," replied the poor man.

"Then," said the official, "I will remind you. Do you remember that some years ago you saved the life of an official in the forest of Warsaw?"

"Yes," replied the man.

"Well, I am that official. Tell me, how did you descend to this situation?"

The poor man related everything that had happened to him. The official took out his pen and wrote him a bill of exchange for two thousand rubles. The man immediately went into business and was very successful, so that in a very short time he returned to his former status.

Meanwhile the tzaddik Reb Elimelekh of Lizhensk had died, the Seer of Lublin filled his place, and Rabbi David of Lelov had also become known as a tzaddik and leader in his generation.

The wealthy man traveled to Rabbi David without knowing that he was the same person he had insulted years earlier. But Rabbi David recognized him immediately when he came to his doorstep, and asked him to tell him everything that had happened to him in the intervening years. The man told him about all the changes that had happened to him.

Rabbi David said to him: "You should know that in the hour you mocked and insulted me, a decree of death for you was declared from Heaven. When I found out about this decree I consulted with Reb Elimelekh about how to cancel the terrible verdict which was decreed against you. We thought of a compromise: that you would become poor, and since 'a poor person is considered dead,' this is how your sin would be atoned for. However, since you had done me such a kindness by bringing me to Lizhensk in your coach, I besought heavenly compassion to grant you clemency, so that after a period of ten years your troubles would end and you would be restored to your former situation."

THE BLESSING OF THE LORD ENRICHES[6]

Reb Elimelekh of Lizhensk once went with another man to immerse in the *mikve.* A heavenly voice was heard saying: "Whoever helps Rabbi Shmelke of Nikolsburg against his opponents who are attacking him is assured of a place in the World to Come."

Reb Elimelekh said to the man accompanying him: "Did you hear a voice just now?"

"No," he replied.

Reb Elimelekh thought to himself: Since I alone heard this voice, it is a sign that I am the one who should go to Nikolsburg.

Reb Elimelekh went to Nikolsburg to see Rabbi Shmelke, and asked his permission to preach in the synagogue and rebuke the congregation. Rabbi Shmelke said to him, "What benefit will come from this, since they do not listen to words of rebuke at all?"

But Reb Elimelekh pleaded with him that nevertheless he should give him permission to preach, until Rabbi Shmelke conceded.

In the synagogue many people gathered to hear the preacher who had come to the city. In his sermon Reb Elimelekh proved to them with false arguments that a number of things forbidden by the Torah are in fact permitted, like the student who found one hundred and fifty ways to declare insects pure. The sermon suited the level of the listeners and was pleasant to their ears. At the end of the sermon Reb Elimelekh announced to the congregation that on the next day he would preach again. The next day almost all the citizens of the city gathered in the synagogue. Reb Elimelekh ascended the pulpit and began to rebuke them with accurate and honest arguments proving that the day before he had not spoken truthfully, and that in fact it is forbidden to transgress not only Torah prohibitions, but also the minor prohibitions from the words of the scribes.

With these words, which came from the heart, Reb Elimelekh put thoughts of *teshuva* in the hearts of all those attending, and they

6. Prov. 10:22.

began to cry, saying to one another, "Is this not the same idea that our rabbi already said to us and we did not want to obey him? We must go now and appease him."

They went to Rabbi Shmelke and prostrated themselves, asking for forgiveness and promising to obey him from then on, since the rebuking preacher had shown them clearly that all his words were true. And Reb Elimelekh took leave of Rabbi Shmelke and went on his way.

As he was leaving Nikolsburg he heard a heavenly voice announcing: "Since you helped Rabbi Shmelke, we are giving you a period of twenty-four hours during which anyone whom you bless will be blessed."

Reb Elimelekh rejoiced over this gift and went on his way. But to his great sorrow, he could not find a Jew to bless. He began to cry before the Blessed One, and said from the depths of his heart: "You have given me a gift of twenty-four hours, but in the end I cannot use it, since I have not encountered a single Jew – so whom shall I bless?"

When he had finished praying to the Blessed One, he saw a woman walking in the field. Reb Elimelekh began to bless her, and she stepped away from him. Reb Elimelekh said to her: "Do not be afraid, since I am not an evil person. Tell me, please, where are you from, and what do you do?" The woman told him about herself, and he blessed her, and went on his way.

The woman came home and told her husband that an unknown man had blessed her on the road. And from that day forward they began to achieve success in their work. They became very wealthy and moved to another city and started large businesses. They were convinced that surely the man who had blessed them was Elijah the prophet.

The man who had grown to be wealthy became very generous. He told his servants that they had permission to give charity up to one gold dinar without informing him, but for more than that they must ask him.

A long time afterward, Reb Elimelekh was traveling with his brother Reb Zusha to collect funds for the redemption of captives. They heard that in a certain city there was a very wealthy and generous man, so they went to see him. When they reached the wealthy man's home the servants wanted to give them a donation of a gold dinar, but they did not want to accept it. The servants said that in order to give more than that amount they would have to ask their master himself. They entered the wealthy man's room, and immediately when his wife saw Reb Elimelekh she fainted from fear. Great confusion reigned in the house. When the woman came round, she said to her husband: "This is Elijah the prophet, who blessed me several years ago, and now he is surely coming to take back from us the wealth that he gave us."

Reb Elimelekh said to them: "Do not fear. I am not Elijah the prophet, and I have not come, Heaven forbid, to take back your wealth. I am a simple Jew. I just blessed you and my blessing was fulfilled."

The wealthy man turned to him with a question: "How much money do you need for the redemption of captives?"

The holy brothers replied that they needed five hundred gold dinars. The wealthy man went and brought them the entire amount, but they did not want to accept it. "We want to leave for others as well the merit of performing this important mitzva," they said. After much pleading by the wealthy man, they received from him half of the amount and left his house in great honor.

A FREE GIFT

One day Reb Elimelekh did an accounting of his soul and came to the conclusion that he had transgressed so much that all seven divisions of *Gehinom* and the bottom levels of Sheol were not enough for him. He was worried and embittered.

While he was examining his soul, five of his holy students came into his room: the Seer of Lublin, the rabbi of Apta, Rabbi Mendel of Rimanov, the Maggid of Kozhnitz, and Rabbi Moshe Leib of Sassov. The rebbe rejoiced on seeing them, and his mind was relieved. He said, "In your merit I hope I will be saved from the judgment of *Gehinom*, since it has been stated: 'The Rabbi will not be in *Gehinom* while his students are in *Gan Eden*...'"

He was still not totally calm. "But how will I receive a place in the World to Come?" he argued with himself.

In the end he encouraged himself with words of comfort, saying: "Nevertheless, do not despair, Elimelekh, and do not let your spirit fall. Even though you are not worthy, you can trust that the Blessed Holy

One will extend to you true kindness and will grant you a place in the World to Come as an exception. For we rely on the words of the holy Talmud[7] that the Blessed Holy One fulfills mitzvot and bestows kindness. And what connection has the bestowing of kindness to the World to Come, where there is no eating or drinking or anything like that? You must say then that giving a place in the World to Come to a person like you is through the quality of *tzedaka* and kindness. Is not the Blessed Holy One the most generous Being in the world, and when we talk about the poverty of the World to Come, behold, I am the poorest of all creatures – and it is clear, therefore, that the Blessed One will give me from His good treasure the treasure of a free gift."

EVEN IN THE HEREAFTER

The day before he died (18 Kislev 5533), the Maggid Rabbi Dov Ber of Mezritch said to his students and his friends: "My children, let unity rule among you. By its strength you will overcome everything. Go upward and not downward. There is a hint to this in the verse 'He is one; who can dissuade Him?'"[8]

After this speech the Maggid sank into a long silence. He seemed to be dozing off. Reb Zusha entered the room on tiptoe. The Maggid awakened and asked, "Who is coming?"

"Zusha is coming," answered Rabbi Shneur Zalman.

The Maggid gestured toward Zusha with his emaciated hand, which moved weakly like a broken wing in a light wind. Reb Zusha approached the bed. The Maggid raised his head from the pillow, and sat up in order to align his face with the eyes of Zusha. The Maggid took the right hand of Reb Zusha and placed his left palm on it, and whispered in a soft voice, yet clearly: "Zusha, you were mine in this world, and even there you will be close to me."

When the Maggid finished speaking, his head dropped on the pillow from exhaustion, but his eyes seemed still fixed on Zusha's face, as if his glance had lifted itself off and was carrying itself, hovering in space, bound in kisses to Zusha.

---

7. Sota 14a.
8. Job 23:13.

Thoughts and Reflections

GREAT THOUGHTS

Under the gem on a woman's jewelry there is a black background,
So that the pearl will shine on the black background,
As the advantage of light over darkness,
As the light stands out from darkness.
And in order that the pearl not be lost in the midst of the black,
And get swallowed into it,
One places under it white threads to heighten it above the black.
But a large pearl does not need white threads,
Since its large size makes it stand out and shine with a great light.
So one must place holy speech and the performance of mitzvot
As white threads under one's thoughts,
In order to elevate them,
Since one's voice and utterances and deeds
Become a chariot for thought.
But the special few great people, whose thoughts are great,
Can connect everything to the oneness in their thought alone.
And they do not need a voice or speech,
Except to bring merit to others and to elevate them with these.

– Reb Elimelekh of Lizhensk

POSITIVE COMMANDMENTS

Reb Elimelekh of Lizhensk would ask his close friends that at every moment of idleness they fix their eyes on the verse "that I may be sanctified in the midst of the Israelite people."[1]

This is how he expressed it: "At every moment when one is free and not occupied in the holy Torah, and especially when one is sitting alone in one's room not doing anything, or lying on one's bed and not sleeping, he should think about the positive command 'that I may be sanctified in the midst of the Israelite people.' One should imagine in one's mind that a great and awesome fire is burning before him, and its flames are rising to heaven, and he, for the sake of the holiness of the name of the Blessed Holy One, breaks his nature and throws himself into the midst of the fire.

"And 'the Blessed Holy One takes a good thought and combines it with the deed,'[2] so that he is not lying or sitting idly but is fulfilling a positive command of the Torah, which is the foundation of the faith and the pillar upon which the entire House of Israel leans."

THOUGHTS OF SIN

"Assail the Midianites and defeat them; for they assailed you by the trickery they practiced against you" (Numbers 25:17–18).
The wickedness of the Midianites was "for they assailed you by the trickery they practiced against you" – in their sinful and impure thoughts with which they infected you.
In this way these non-Jews became tricksters tied to the Jewish people.
Ḥazal already taught: "Thoughts of sin are worse than sin itself."[3]
This rule is valid in all places and in all times.
For if one tempts another to commit an act of transgression or evil,
One can make it right through repentance and good deeds.
But one who remains with false ideas and with faulty opinions – it cannot be made right.
"Whoever goes to her (evil ideas) cannot return and find again the paths of life."[4]
– Reb Elimelekh of Lizhensk

1. Lev. 22:32.
2. Kiddushin 40a.
3. Yoma 29a.
4. Prov. 2:19.

Torah Study

TORAH AND FIRE

The Torah was given with fire,
In order that we may know that one must fulfill it
With the fire of enthusiasm and dedication.

– Reb Elimelekh of Lizhensk

THE RIGHTEOUS ONE

It was not necessary to add to Reb Zusha's name any title, for example HaRav Reb Zusha, or the tzaddik Reb Zusha, or the scholar, the pious, or the miracle worker. His name was his title. Every tzaddik had his own special place or his own beit midrash within the sanctuary of Hasidism, while Reb Zusha was always wandering without a roof over his head.

It is the way of the world that a person's soul will carry him far away to reach new places, to mix with different people in order to examine their actions or to learn from their customs. And there are some who wish to teach and to influence, and since one cannot be a good teacher or advisor in his own city, against his will he wanders and goes to places where they do not know him. Some are wanderers in their youth out of love, because the dust of the roads is pleasant to them, or they believe that the afflictions of travel will atone for the sins of their youth.

On the other hand, when they grow older they wish to dwell in their houses and to see sweet rest; they desire their own space, to observe a set way of life, to be masters among their people, to set a table, especially in grand style, and if they are fortunate, they reach the rank of leaders and managers.

This was not the case with Reb Zusha, who was a perennial youth, a lifelong wanderer; he never became an *Admor* or leader of a community, since he did not desire anything like that. The issue never entered his mind; it was not in the calculations of the righteous and holy Zusha, a truly humble person who had no idea that he was humble, who was always filled with love of the Creator, who had not an iota of concern in his soul for any caprice in this world. Since he was a vessel totally filled with love and longing for the Eternal, it did not occur to him to declare himself a rabbi. The lips of all the tzaddikim whisper in their graves because people speak in their name words of Torah, sayings of wisdom and piety, but there are not many teachings and lessons from Reb Zusha. Reb Zusha said almost nothing. He was just Reb Zusha.

REB ZUSHA TEACHES A DEVAR TORAH

When Reb Zusha was young, it was his custom to speak words of Torah at his table with great fervor, before large crowds listening to words of the living God. But in his mature years he began to be careful to guard his words. He would speak only occasionally, and even then only at a favorable time. And so his Torah discussions diminished, to the point that he reached a level of almost total silence.

It happened once that Reb Zusha and his *gabbai,* Reb Leibush, came to a certain city on the day before the holy Shabbat. At evening the leaders of the city and many important men came to his inn who convinced Reb Leibush to persuade Reb Zusha to teach some Torah at their table. Reb Zusha covered his face with his hands and said: "Did you hear, Zusha? The *gabbai* Leibush is asking me in the name of the leaders of the city to teach some Torah. I am surprised: What do you have to teach, Zusha?"

Reb Zusha did not say a word, and the leaders of the city left. Only workers and a few poor folk remained at the table. They had not dared to beg Reb Zusha at first, nor did they now.

in the presence of the trees in the forest? Reb Leibush was right to be angry, both for the loss of the gold pieces that would have been used for the welfare of the indigent tzaddikim, and also for what he himself had lost, since the monthly leader had promised to drop a coin in his pocket if the rabbi would preach in their city.

When Reb Zusha finished, Reb Leibush dared to say to him: "I am surprised at the rabbi, since he refused to speak before a congregation of Jews in the city."

Reb Zusha replied: "What is the sin and what is the transgression of Zusha? Zusha cannot speak unless He, as it were, wants him to speak."

Reb Zusha was quiet for a short while, and then said: "When Zusha was young in years and young in mind, he was a flowing spring, like a river that does not stop, and he spoke words of Torah at all opportunities. When people would come to him wanting to hear him, he belonged to the community. When Zusha grew up and matured a little, he was not accustomed anymore to speak when others wanted to hear him, except when a strong excitement seized him to teach the community. Zusha the wicked belonged then only to Zusha. Then he got older, and Zusha the elder belonged not to the community and not to Zusha, but was devoted completely and solely to the Master of the Universe. And again he was not permitted to teach Torah except when the Blessed One desired. Zusha of the Blessed One is not suited at all to teach Torah before important and wealthy people, who press the Divine Presence in their arrogance."

But Reb Leibush was persistent. "Nevertheless, I am surprised, Rabbi. Before whom does the rabbi now teach new interpretations of the Torah?"

Reb Zusha replied: "Leibush, Leibush, do you not understand what Zusha the wicked understands? Torah which is taught even in the field, in a forest, or in an inner chamber, they hear it, they hear it, everyone hears it, since whoever has ears to hear will hear it, as it is written in the holy Torah: "Both those who are standing here with us this day... and those who are not with us here this day."[1]

---

1. Deut. 29:14.

ENDORSEMENT

When people came to Reb Zusha to obtain from him an endorsement for the *Tanya,* he ordered to have a lot of paper brought to his desk. No matter how many sheets of paper they brought, he still asked for more.

But when he dipped his quill into the inkwell, he said: "Enough; do not bring any more, since no matter how many sheets of paper you bring, it will not be enough to describe the praiseworthy qualities of this book. It would be better, therefore, to suffice with a small piece of paper." Therefore Reb Zusha's endorsement at the front of the *Tanya* is very short.

THE SCHOLAR

Reb Elimelekh was forty-three years old when Rabbi Yisrael Baal Shem Tov died. Both for him and for his brother Zusha, there had been many opportunities to leave Lithuania, their birthplace, and to go and seek him out. But they did not. Perhaps this was because Lithuania, the stronghold of the *mitnagdim* (opponents of Hasidism), was closed tightly against Hasidism for an even longer time than Poland and Ukraine.

Only a little is known about the years before they affiliated with Hasidism. We know that their mother, a pious widow even though she was not educated – she could not read the prayer book although she knew all the prayers by heart – was a central influence in their early development. We also know that Reb Elimelekh's desire was for the Talmud, while Zusha leaned toward contemplation and meditation. It was probably the case that when he heard a wandering preacher tell stories and talk about miracles that one could see and experience in Mezritch, he decided to travel there, seeking not learning or wisdom but ardor and redemption.

While Reb Elimelekh occupied himself with the study and interpretation of the complicated structure of Talmudic concepts and arguments, Zusha spent his days and nights wandering in the forests, dancing and singing to God. To his brother he explained: "I am like a servant who loves his king but who can see him only through a hole in the wall. You resemble the prince who is permitted to tarry near the king on condition that he study the art of using words."

In its early days Hasidism was taught orally, and its essential strength was in the personal living contact between the teacher and the pupil. Torah scholars and masses of simple men listened to the sermons of the tzaddik, and each of them absorbed the words according to his spiritual ability – the scholars according to their level, the simple folk according to their level. The students of the Besht would say: "Whoever has heard a word of Torah from the mouth of our master will never forget it."

In the book *Maor VaShemesh,* by Rabbi Kalonymus HaLevi Epstein of Kraków, it is said that Reb Elimelekh would stand outside someone's house and say words of Torah while the people sat around him in a circle. And when he told a story, the heart of all his listeners was torn into twelve pieces, and each one thought that the rabbi directed the story to him. The feeling that every student felt that his words were directed to him and to him alone came from the living speech that issued from the mouth of the teacher and from the voice that accompanied the words.

HOW I LOVE YOUR TORAH[2]

It happened that a Hasid of Reb Elimelekh lingered in the court of his rabbi weeks and months, and after he returned to his city his hasidic friends asked him during the *Seuda Shlishit* (the third Shabbat meal) to repeat the words of Torah that he had heard from the rabbi at the Shabbat table.

The Hasid thought about it and said: "The rabbi spoke words of Torah that enlivened our souls. But it will not profit you for me to review them. The rabbi did not say in his teaching one-thousandth of what he thought. I only understood from his words one-thousandth of what I heard. I can only transmit to you one-thousandth of what I understood. You will understand only one-thousandth of what I say. Now go and calculate the amount that you will gain if I repeat the Torah which I heard."

UNTIL MIDNIGHT

It was the custom of Reb Elimelekh to go to bed in the early evening and to sleep until midnight. From then on he would occupy himself all night with study of Torah and with prayer. He would say that the Torah study and the prayers rise to heaven only after midnight.

---

2. Ps. 119:97.

When Reb Elimelekh arose from his sleep he would sigh and say: "Woe is me and woe is my life! I spent my time sleeping for nothing and for no reward."

And Rabbi Mendel of Rimanov would say: "On the day before the holy Shabbat after immersing in the *mikve,* I can understand a passage in the book *Noam Elimelekh* written by Reb Elimelekh of Lizhensk."

Truth and Falsehood

THE PRICE OF A LIE

Even one falsehood
Will keep you far from the Holy Blessed One,
Because the speaker of lies cannot stand firm before His eyes.

– Reb Zusha of Anipoli

BOTH THESE AND THOSE ARE WORDS OF TRUTH

One Erev Shabbat Reb Elimelekh was sitting in a tub of hot water in the bathhouse. Along came a certain Jew who was not from the local city, and also entered the bathtub to wash himself in honor of Shabbat.

Reb Elimelekh asked him, "From where have you come?"

The man replied, "I came to Lizhensk from Hungary in order to merit seeing the shining light, the great tzaddik, Reb Elimelekh."

Reb Elimelekh asked him, "Have you seen Elimelekh yet?"

The man replied angrily, "Why are you speaking disrespectfully of the holy rabbi, the greatest tzaddik in the world? You don't refer to him as 'Elimelekh' but rather 'Reb Elimelekh,' may he live a long and good life. Reb Elimelekh is the tzaddik of this generation."

Reb Elimelekh asked him, "Does falsehood reign even in your country, Hungary, so that there too Elimelekh the sinner is well known as the tzaddik of the generation?"

When the visitor heard his neighbor in the bath insulting Reb Elimelekh, he rebuked him and said: "Shut your mouth, you evil person! You are insulting the honor of one of God's angels. You should be torn apart like a fish, such an arrogant and insolent one as you."

The visitor finished bathing, immersed in the *mikve,* dried himself, and got dressed. He returned to his inn dressed for Shabbat, reviewed the weekly Torah reading, and went to meet Reb Elimelekh. When he entered Reb Elimelekh's study, he went into shock.

Reb Elimelekh asked him, "Reb Yid, why are you upset?"

The visitor replied with restrained tears: "Woe is me! I am the one who insulted the honor of your holiness when we were together in the bath. Woe is me that I have opened my mouth against God's holy servant. I acted so foolishly! I lacked the common sense to recognize with whom I was sitting in the bath."

"Relax, Reb Yid," Reb Elimelekh comforted him. "What I said in the bath about Elimelekh, and what you said there, are both words of truth."

AN OUNCE OF TRUTH

It happened once that Rabbi Gavriel of Chortkov in the Ukraine hired a wagon to travel to see Reb Elimelekh. The wagon driver was coarse in his speech and in his behavior and caused him much embarrassment. Nevertheless, wonder of of wonders, when he arrived in Lizhensk Reb Elimelekh welcomed the driver joyfully and with affection.

Some days later Rabbi Gavriel came with the wagon driver to an inn in Lvov, and there the wagon driver met with a skilled builder. Rabbi Gavriel noticed that there was great affection between the wagon driver and the artisan. The two of them sat by themselves in a corner, whispering to each other. He approached them unobtrusively and heard a little bit of their conversation. They were saying that in these times there is an ounce of truth, but it is found only with Reb Elimelekh and nowhere else.

When they noticed that he was listening to them, they berated him, saying, "What does a rabbi and a scholar like you want with simple folks like us?"

A short while later Reb Elimelekh died. After his death Rabbi Gavriel and Rabbi Uri of Strelisk went to visit Reb Zusha in Anipoli. On the way Rabbi Gavriel related to Rabbi Uri what he had heard from the two simple fellows about Reb Elimelekh's ounce of truth.

The two of them burst into tears and said, "Alas, there was only an ounce of truth in the world, and even that was taken from us."

Rabbi Gavriel stood under one tree, and Rabbi Uri stood under another tree, and they both sobbed harder and harder until the wagon driver urged them to get into the wagon.

HIS PORTION IS ASSURED

Reb Elimelekh said to himself: "I am certain that I have a place reserved for myself in the World to Come. When I shall come before the heavenly court and they will ask me: 'Were you involved with studying Torah as commanded?' I will answer: 'No.'

"Next they will ask me: 'Did you offer your regular prayers as commanded?' Again I will reply: 'No.'

"Next they will ask: 'Were you involved in good deeds as commanded?' Once again I will have to give the same answer.

"They will immediately deliver the judgment: 'You speak the truth. For the sake of the truth you are assured a place in the World to Come.'"

Nevertheless Reb Elimelekh impressed on his students: "If the heavenly court metes out a judgment that I must go down to *Gehinom,* I shall ask them: 'In whose name do you pronounce this judgment?' And they will answer me: 'In the name of Hashem.' Then I will jump into the netherworld with all my might, eagerly and enthusiastically, because in doing so I shall be fulfilling the command of the Blessed Holy One."

WHAT BENEFIT IS THERE IN THIS?

A man named Reb Avraham, a deeply pious Jew, made a very good living from his store. Toward the end of his life, he thought about his career in business and began to feel regret and guilt that he had spent all his life making a living, had ignored Torah study, and had had little time for prayer. He consulted his partner in life, a woman of valor, and with her agreement began to set aside time every day for Torah study and more lengthy prayer. He also drew near to Reb Elimelekh of Lizhensk, in whose presence he sat often, studying *musar* and proper behavior.

It happened once that Reb Avraham heard Reb Elimelekh strongly denounce the sin of lying, a sin committed by many. Reb Elimelekh went so far as to claim that even an accidental falsehood creates a flaw in the soul. By contrast, the rabbi praised truthfulness to the skies and stated that there is rarely a blessing as great as truth. There is no mitzva as precious as this, such that even the wicked King Jeroboam ben Nebat was guaranteed a place in the World to Come because he had spent twenty-four consecutive hours without lying.

Reb Avraham decided to separate himself from everyone, even from his family, for twenty-four consecutive hours. He closeted himself in a special room in his house to be alone for a full day. Worried that if he engaged in conversation with anyone he might accidentally speak something that had a slight taint of falsehood, he locked the door to his room, and ordered his family not to come in nor admit anyone else for the next twenty-four hours.

He wrapped himself in tallis and tefillin and did not pause for a minute from his studies. He even refrained from sleeping all night, lest he have wayward dreams whose content might be lies, and it would turn out that he was harboring untruths in his heart.

The next morning, before he had finished his isolation of twenty-four hours, he heard a knocking on his door and the voice of a non-Jew. He hurried to answer since his family was still asleep, and he did not want the knocking to awaken them. He opened the door, and there stood a non-Jew who said to him, "Give me a shovel. I need a shovel."

"I don't have a shovel in the house," answered Reb Avraham.

The non-Jew laughed: "Maybe you have a shovel but do not want to give it to me?"

Reb Avraham replied: "I don't have a shovel."

The non-Jew pressed again: "Maybe you have a shovel, and you are lying about the shovel?"

Reb Avraham replied: "Really, I don't have a shovel in my house."

The non-Jew gave him an amazed look, and said angrily: "You are a liar, Jew, a total liar. You don't know that yesterday toward evening I passed by here near your house, and I had a shovel in my hand. I was thirsty for a drink and wanted to go to a tavern, but I didn't have even a small coin. I asked your wife to lend me a little money. She was afraid I would not return the loan, so I gave her my shovel for security. I went to the tavern and drank some wine, but I didn't pay – I lied and said that I didn't have any money. I was afraid that I would not be able to collect the debt the next morning, and the shovel is important to me for work in the morning, so I came now. Here, take the money, Jew, and return my shovel!"

Just then his wife woke up, came to the door, and returned the shovel to the non-Jew.

Reb Avraham was very distressed that he had lost his place in the World to Come because of his accidental untruth. He wanted to express his sorrow to Reb Elimelekh, but when he went to him he could not. Because of his deep feelings, he was unable to speak. He kept trying, without success, until Reb Elimelekh turned his face toward him and asked him: "Did you fail, Reb Avraham?"

"Rabbi, woe is me, the shovel, the shovel… woe is me, the shovel caused me to fail." He fell silent and did not explain further.

Reb Elimelekh encouraged him with a smiling face, saying: "It seems that you stumbled and told an accidental untruth because of the shovel, but an accidental untruth does not constitute an intentional crime. Sometimes the Blessed Holy One causes a Jew to stumble in order to teach him, or to warn him about something in the Torah or about proper behavior."

This encouraged Reb Avraham and reduced his distress a bit. He related to Reb Elimelekh what had happened with the shovel of the non-Jewish man.

Reb Elimelekh smiled and said: "You see, Reb Avraham, God has many messengers to teach a Jew common sense. The Besht taught that everything can be a lesson from Heaven. Every voice that one hears can be a divine voice from above. Even this shovel can be a sign from God to unearth a positive moral trait in the Torah and in fear of God, or in good moral habits. The Blessed Holy One wanted to teach you, Reb Avraham, that this is not an occasion to abandon your business or to go into hiding, to leave your commerce and drop all your financial burdens on your wife. Your wife is only your helpmate; she is not obliged to bear the weight of your sustenance.

"Our ancient rabbis taught in *Pirkei Avot,* 'Worthy is Torah study together with a worldly occupation.' You must understand, Reb Avraham, that had you not isolated yourself from the responsibilities of your household in order to be alone for twenty-four hours so that you could acquire in a short time a place in the World to Come, you would have known that you had received a shovel for security, and you would not have fallen prey to an accidental falsehood. Is there any benefit in avoiding falsehood through isolation from the world? There is advantage in being engaged with people while being careful to avoid a falsehood. Only one who deals faithfully in business so as to pass twenty-four consecutive hours without lying is indeed assured of a place in the World to Come."

KEEP YOUR DISTANCE

"Keep far from falsehood" (Exodus 23:7).
Speaking lies is the only transgression in the Torah for which it is not sufficient only to avoid it,
But one must also keep a great distance from it.
In connection with no other transgression are we commanded to distance ourselves from it.

– Reb Zusha of Anipoli

Tzaddik

THREE KINDS OF TZADDIKIM

It is written in the book of Numbers, in *Parashat Naso,* that the Blessed One commanded Moshe to appoint the family of Gershon and the families of Kehat and Merari for service in the Sanctuary.

This is a hint that there are three kinds of tzaddikim, each on a different level. There is a tzaddik who is called "Kehat," from the phrase "*velo yikhat amim* (the homage of the people will be his),"[1] because the collection of (*kehilat*) his good deeds will serve to teach humanity the ways of goodness. There is a tzaddik in the category of "Merari,"[2] who punishes himself with bitter afflictions in fear and self-denial. And there is a tzaddik who is in the category of "Gershon,"[3] namely, a stranger in the land, humble and modest, despised and loathsome in his own eyes.

These are the three levels of holiness.

– Reb Elimelekh of Lizhensk

THE ROLE OF THE TZADDIK

Reb Elimelekh had a complex character. His brother Zusha was of a single nature. Zusha was Zusha all the time; he did not ask to be someone

1. Gen. 49:10.
2. The name "Merari" has the letters of the word "*mar* (bitter)."
3. See Ex. 2:22.

else. Reb Elimelekh wanted to be both Elimelekh and Zusha. In that way he could simultaneously preach joy and live a life of monasticism, be trapped by the external savor of power and at the same time reject it, put his hand in a burning fire and oppose self-mortification. Like many tzaddikim after him, he lived a double life. Publicly he walked a path that followed the ways of the Besht, while in his private life he wandered in the confusion of pain and suffering.

However, he never went so far as to suggest that the average Hasid must try to go in his footsteps. In his court the tzaddikim of Apta, Lublin, Ropshitz, Rimanov, and Kozhnitz learned that they had to be accessible to their Hasidim at all times and on every subject. They learned how to take part in the lives of their Hasidim, to be interested in their business affairs, to help arrange their marriages, to reconcile conflicts among them, and to organize the collection of *tzedaka* to pay their debts.

Reb Elimelekh taught them the art of counseling in times of crisis, and how to shake up the comfortable and to comfort the afflicted. Staying in Lizhensk meant being totally involved with the rabbi and the Hasid alike. "Being alone is not a solution," said Reb Elimelekh. "Instead of being alone with yourself, be alone with your thoughts." Among Lizhensk-style Hasidism there was total care by every Hasid for his friends.

Instead of teaching his Hasidim Kabbala or theology, Reb Elimelekh gave them a copy of his "Tzetel Katan," a short list of small acts they should perform every day, upon arising in the morning, when praying, when doing business, when alone or with others. It was an enumeration of seventeen points which directed one how to be a good Jew with a minimum of effort. He left the theology to the tzaddikim. The Hasidim required simple answers to questions that were not so simple.

It is told that the involvement of Reb Elimelekh in the lives of his Hasidim was such that one could sense it immediately. Whoever saw him or was seen near him carried him in his heart. No one ever passed through Lizhensk without being changed.

THE TZADDIK AS REBUKER AT THE GATE

Among the students of the Maggid of Mezritch, Reb Elimelekh was considered to be a rebuker. Hasidim of the Besht style were not comfortable with the *maggidim* (preachers) who in their sermons would preach ethics and make accusations against the Jews. The great masters of Hasidism especially were not pleased with those *maggidim* who, after preaching their sermons in the beit midrash, would go out and knock on doors asking for donations as a reward for their sermon. "When they chastise the community in order to receive afterward a fee for their rebukes," said one of the great rabbis of Hasidism, "these words of rebuke do not come from the heart and do not enter the hearts of their listeners."

However, Reb Elimelekh possessed a different quality. He would behave like his brother Reb Zusha, who would castigate himself and not others. When Reb Elimelekh reached a certain city and heard that its citizens were making light of halakhic Shabbat observance, he would immediately ask the beadles of the community to gather the people in the beit midrash, and in their presence ascend the pulpit and begin to rebuke himself.

He would say: "Elimelekh, woe unto you on the Day of Judgment, woe unto you on the day of admonition! You disregard the halakhic observance of Shabbat, and you do not understand at all the value of the sanctity of the Shabbat. How great is the reward of one who sanctifies the Shabbat properly, and how great is the punishment of one who desecrates the Shabbat."

In this way he would begin to explain to the crowd of listeners the importance of the Shabbat in all its details and features, its holiness and its beauty, turning his two shining eyes toward heaven, and would mention in passing a few teachings of our sages in the Talmud, in the midrash, and in the Zohar about the attributes of the Shabbat and the greatness of its value, and all of it with enthusiasm and inspiration, and with all kinds of explanation, without offending the honor of anyone. The rebuke was directed toward himself, the one who did not observe Shabbat properly. They all listened attentively, opening wide their mouths and swallowing every word and utterance, countless eyes fixed on Reb Elimelekh, their hearts moved with great fear. The rebuke worked its magic....

WHAT'S MINE IS YOURS AND WHAT'S YOURS IS YOURS

"Noah was a righteous man; he was blameless in his age; Noah walked with God" (Genesis 6:9).

Reb Elimelekh of Lizhensk taught this parable: "What does this resemble? There are two ways to get warm when it is freezing cold. One can light a fire in the stove, or one can wrap oneself in furs. By lighting the stove one warms oneself and others, but by wrapping onself in fur one warms only oneself – the others are still cold.

"A tzaddik who worries only about warming himself and does not care about warming the whole world – he is nothing but a *tzaddik in peltz* (a tzaddik in a warm coat), and not a complete tzaddik."

A TREACHEROUS BREED[4]

Reb Zusha of Anipoli would say: "We learn in Midrash Rabba *(Parashat Va'era)*: "In the future *Gan Eden* will be shouting: 'Give me tzaddikim; I have no interest in evil people.' And in the future *Gehinom* will be shouting: 'I have no interest in tzaddikim.' So it seems that the matter is questionable: Why this shouting? How can one think that tzaddikim are brought to *Gehinom*, and evil people to *Gan Eden*?

"The only way to understand it," he added, "is that in the future it will be difficult to distinguish between a tzaddik and an evil person, and the angels will be mistaken, bringing evil people to *Gan Eden* and tzaddikim to *Gehinom*, and both of them – *Gan Eden* and *Gehinom* – will have to shout a warning, so that there should be no mistakes, Heaven forbid, in the reckoning."

IN A WHISPER AND IN A SHOUT

There is a tzaddik who can act and pray in a whisper, and every utterance makes an impression. And there is a tzaddik who is not on that level, so he must pray by shouting to the Blessed One.

– Reb Elimelekh of Lizhensk

THE TZADDIKIM THEMSELVES ARE SURPRISED

"When Pharaoh speaks to you and says, 'Produce for you a miracle,' you shall say to Aharon, 'Take your rod and cast it down before Pharaoh.' It will turn into a serpent" (Exodus 7:9).

4. Deut. 32:20.

"Produce for you a miracle"? It should have been written, "Produce for us a miracle." It may be said that when miracles are produced by magicians and sorcerers, only the onlookers are surprised, since the magician himself knows that this is nothing more than deception and delusion. But with miracles performed by prophets and tzaddikim, which are from divine power, they themselves are surprised by the revelation of the miracle.

So it says, "Produce for you a miracle," because even "for you" it will be a miracle.

– Reb Elimelekh of Lizhensk

Tzedaka

FORGIVE ME, PARDON ME

In a certain inn a wealthy guest mistook Reb Zusha for a beggar and treated him accordingly. After a while Reb Zusha's true identity became known to him, and he came crying to Reb Zusha. "Forgive me, Rabbi. You must forgive me, since I did not know!"

"Why do you ask forgiveness from Zusha?" said Reb Zusha, nodding his head and smiling. "You did not do anything wrong to him. You did not insult Zusha, but a poor beggar. Go therefore and ask beggars everywhere to forgive you."

TWO POCKETS

When I travel to collect money for *tzedaka,*
I take with me two pockets,
One for the insults,
And the other for the money.

– Reb Zusha of Anipoli

THE FOUR CORNERS OF THE EARTH

When a person goes to the four corners of the earth
To collect *tzedaka* for the poor,
He is forgiven through this for the four kinds of death decreed by the court.

– Reb Elimelekh of Lizhensk

Wealth

WEALTH

Wealth, like Torah and vows,
Needs a fence around it to protect it.
One needs to know how to deal with it
And how to live with it.
In wealth, one can attain much,
But one also can lose much.

– Reb Elimelekh of Lizhensk

THE INHERITANCE

The father of Reb Zusha and Reb Elimelekh, Rabbi Eliezer Lipman, was an affluent Jewish villager who lived with wealth and died with a good name, leaving his seven children a large inheritance which was divided among them. His money he gave to his son Avraham, his fields and houses to his son Natan, his jewels and furniture to Elimelekh, and the money he was owed from debtors he left to Zusha.

Thus, by the irony of fate, Zusha the simple and honest, who could not hurt a fly on a wall, who asked nothing for himself, who never came with a claim for anything, was found to be the right one, as it were, to be assertive with debtors, who generally are not eager to pay, and how much less so to pay the heirs of a creditor.

Who was responsible for this ironic situation? The father in bequeathing his property? The sons in dividing the inheritance among themselves, in scheming by a secret agreement to deprive their simple brother, the unsuccessful one, to give him something that is not actually given, but has to be claimed or even taken by force? Was it life itself that decreed the details of the division of the inheritance, or perhaps the clever imagination of the storyteller who made up this joke? But the stamp of truth is imprinted on this detail, whether it's the truth of legend or the truth of reality. There is no reality like the reality of legends.

Zusha, the way he is, is the way he is dealt with. For Zusha, who has surrendered Zusha, as he is, in body and soul, it is fitting and fine for him to give up his share of the inheritance, and to receive in exchange a share which is just a claim, and which in the future is likely to involve him in complex difficulties, in insults and abuse, in the tawdriness of the courts and in the abomination of disputes, and maybe even some good, hard beatings.

Thus, Reb Zusha was very poor. He was often nagged by his wife.

He said to her once, "Imagine if I were wealthy, but a miser. Even then we would not be living very comfortably."

HIS PRAYER WAS ANSWERED

In his final days on earth, Reb Elimelekh turned to his family and said that he was praying that his children would not become wealthy, so that they would walk on the righteous path and not come to bad behavior.

"Abba," answered one of his children, "will you not in this way cause people to speak ill of you, Heaven forbid, since the Talmud teaches: 'The righteous man who prospers is a righteous son of a righteous man'; whereas 'the righteous man who is in adversity is a righteous man son of a wicked man'?[1] If our situation worsens, they will say, Heaven forbid, that our father was not a tzaddik!"

Reb Elimelekh smiled and said that now he understood the midrash on the verse "Yitzḥak pleaded with the Lord...."[2] The midrash states: "Yitzḥak pleaded – this teaches that he poured out his heart in

1. Berakhot 7a.
2. Gen. 25:21.

prayer abundantly (which can also mean he prayed for abundance)."[3] How is it possible to say that our father Yitzḥak, who despised all the vanities of this world and laid down his life to God, requested abundance?

Rather, because "the scoffers of the generation said: Sarah became pregnant from Avimelekh," Yitzḥak said to the Blessed Holy One: "How can I prove to the whole world that I am the son of Avraham? If you will give me wealth and property, then whether I am a tzaddik or an evil person, Heaven forbid, in any case the wealth that you will give me will be a sign that I am the son of a tzaddik, since 'The righteous man who prospers is a righteous son of a righteous man, and an evil person who prospers is an evil son of a righteous man.' But if you decree poverty for me, then whether I am a righteous person or an evil person, they will say that I am the son of the evil Avimelekh, since 'a righteous person whose finances worsen is a righteous son of an evil man, and an evil person whose finances worsen is an evil son of an evil father.'" Therefore he prayed to the Almighty to grant him prosperity.

The Hasidim who tell this story emphasize that nevertheless Reb Elimelekh did not change his request, and to this day none of his descendants has been wealthy.

"AND THE MONEY ANSWERS EVERYTHING"

"Men who fear God, trustworthy men who scorn dishonest gain" (Exodus 18:21).
Regarding all the other qualities of which the leaders of the people must be innocent, it is stated only in a general way: "men who fear God, trustworthy men."
Only one shameful quality does the Torah point out in detail: "those who scorn dishonest gain,"
Since this is the most evil of all appetites.
No appetite is so deeply rooted and persistent,
And there is no appetite as difficult to uproot as the appetite for dishonest gain.

– Reb Zusha of Anipoli

---

3. Gen. Rabba 63.

Man's Inclinations

LITTLE BY LITTLE

Once Reb Zusha and Reb Elimelekh went on a journey and arrived at an inn. Reb Zusha entered the inn to see what kind of place it was, while Reb Elimelekh stood outside and waited for him. Reb Zusha tarried inside for a whole hour, so Reb Elimelekh came in to see what was the reason for his delay. He found his brother standing and looking at a pair of drunken farmers begging the bartender to give them another drink.

"What do you see, my brother?" asked Reb Elimelekh.

"I am observing the ways of the evil inclination," answered Reb Zusha.

The farmer stood there drunk, his wife beside him, pleading with him to stop, since it was the season of threshing in the field, and there was much work to be done, and time was passing quickly. The farmer refused and coaxed her to taste the liquor. He continued trying to persuade her until she was enticed, and she tasted, and tasted again, and she became drunk – and now she too was begging the bartender for more liquor.

"Is this not the method of the evil inclination, my brother? First it coaxes one to taste a little bit, then one listens to it, and in the end one runs after it."

A CONVERSATION WITH THE EVIL INCLINATION

It happened once that Reb Elimelekh heard the evil inclination speaking to him, and this is what it said:

"I am warning you, Elimelekh, not to keep preaching *musar* (Jewish ethics) to everyone and leading them on the right path. Because if you bring everyone in the world to goodness, what will be left for me to do? No one will need me, and I will be good for nothing. But if you do not obey me and continue in the future to be a teacher of righteousness and good deeds, you should know, Elimelekh, that I will ignore everyone else, and will focus only on you. And if I battle only with you, and with no one else, how will you defeat me?"

Reb Elimelekh answered him: "I will in no way obey you. In any case you do everything in your power to divert me from the good path and lure me toward transgressions. You are not partial to anyone. So what I can do in order to save misguided souls from your cunning, I will continue to do."

LOWER YOURSELF

"Make for Me an altar of earth and sacrifice on it your burnt offerings and your sacrifices of well-being" (Exodus 20:21).
If you desire to sacrifice your evil inclination,
Make yourself like the earth, lowly and worthless, like dust and ashes.
"And sacrifice on it your burnt offerings...."
In that way you will sacrifice all the powers of evil which arise to tempt you.
"And your sacrifices of well-being" – and thus you will come to achieve well-being.

– Reb Elimelekh of Lizhensk

The fonts used in this book are from the Arno family

Menorah Books
Jewish Life & Spirituality in Practice
Koren Publishers Jerusalem Ltd.